LS3P

THE MASTER ARCHITECT SERIES V

LS3P ASSOCIATES LTD.

Selected and Current Works

First published in Australia in 2002
by The Images Publishing Group Pty Ltd
ACN 059 734 431
6 Bastow Place, Mulgrave, Victoria, 3170
Telephone (61 3) 9561 5544 Facsimile (61 3) 9561 4860
Email: books@images.com.au
Website: www.imagespublishinggroup.com

National Library of Australia
Cataloguing-in-Publication data

LS3P ASSOCIATES LTD.: selected and current works

Includes index.
ISBN 1 876907 77 0.

1. LS3P Associates. 2. Architecture - United States - 20th
century. 3. Architecture, American. I. Title. (Series :
Master architect series. V).

720.973

Edited by Fiona Gruber
Designed by The Graphic Image Studio Pty Ltd, Mulgrave, Australia
Film separations by SC (Sang Choy) International Pte Ltd, Singapore
Printed by Everbest Printing Co. Ltd. in Hong Kong/China

Contents

Introduction
LS3P ASSOCIATES LTD.

By Frank E. Lucas, FAIA, Chairman

From a one-man, one-room office in May of 1963, in Charleston, South Carolina, a vibrant, aggressive, design-conscious, service-oriented multi-disciplined architectural firm has emerged. Poised to celebrate forty years of practice in 2003, LS3P ASSOCIATES LTD., with a staff of more than 160, and over 100 design awards, looks to a very bright future.

In 1964, Frank E. Lucas, FAIA, was joined in practice by Sidney W. Stubbs, Jr., FAIA, to become Lucas and Stubbs Associates Ltd. In a basement office that flooded regularly at full-moon tides, the two young but determined architects completed the required drawings for a 2,700-seat auditorium and exhibition hall competition in ankle-deep sea water. Daytime was reserved for current projects, leaving only the very late hours for the competition effort. Working barefooted with rolled up trousers and wrinkled drawings, they submitted the winning design. The building later received an AIA Design Award. The success of the first major project set the standards for the future. Design, service, integrity, and responsiveness became the essence of the practice. From the very beginning of the firm, commitment and enthusiasm were what clients saw and associated with Lucas and Stubbs. Most projects were from repeat clients, more than pleased with previous efforts.

In 1982 Vito Pascullis, Richard Powell, and Thom Penney became partners in the firm, renamed Lucas, Stubbs, Pascullis, Powell and Penney, Ltd. LS3P became the popular name and later the legal title.

LS3P is a larger and stronger organization now, yet everyone who works with them still has that same sense of urgency and commitment to every design challenge. Vito, Richard, and Thom have certainly demonstrated those qualities during the years they have been with the firm. Their leadership has been invaluable to the firm; not only as studio leaders, but as shapers of our growth and management. We have served our clients well.

Thom Penney, FAIA, who came to the firm as a part-time high school student, worked with LS3P throughout his Bachelor's and Master's program at Clemson University. He assumed the Presidency of LS3P in 1989. Thom's vision and management skills have added immeasurably to its organizational strengths and quality of services. From the very beginning of the practice, the culture of LS3P has been one of loyalty, integrity, and commitment to 'do the right thing for the right reasons.' Throughout its forty year history, that same level of responsibility has been the focus of the firm's work and character.

The year 1999 brought major change to LS3P. TBA[2], of Charlotte, North Carolina, a 60-person architectural firm, merged with LS3P, bringing an enhanced history of investment and commercial facilities, and industrial design. Mike Tribble, FAIA, became the Vice Chairman and Managing Principal of LS3P in Charlotte. The combined histories of the two firms became far stronger than the two separate organizations. A greater geographic service area, a near perfect meshing of expertise, project type, and more importantly, almost identical firm cultures made LS3P into one of the Southeast's strongest design firms. Project delivery capabilities were broadened. An already significant client base was better served and expanded.

In 2000, Vito Pascullis, AIA, retired, and Susan Baker, AIA, became Chief Operations Officer and relocated from Charleston to Charlotte. Tom Hund, AIA, became Principal-in-Charge of the Charleston Office of LS3P. Barbara Price, AIA, became Principal-in-Charge of the Charlotte operation in 2002.

A reorganization of service teams divided the practice into segments, with either project types, client leaders (or both) as division types. The firm is still growing and still finding ways to better serve its clients.

The teams and divisions are:

community – land planning

enterprise – investment

discovery – health care/research

knowledge – education

image – interiors

pantecta – special services

metropolis – urban

exploration – civic

performance – federal

The LS3P organizational structure enables our staff to serve clients more personally and more professionally. We are large enough to have total design capabilities from site selection through interior design and complementary expanded services, all within the firm. And we are small enough to give personal attention while drawing off the total resources of the firm. All projects are under the direct control of a Principal and a Client Leader, who assemble a project design team on the basis of relevant skills, experience, and compatibility with the particular client.

LS3P has examined the typical architectural practice to determine where shortfalls occur, and where most client complaints arise. Traditionally, in the profession, complaints come from several areas, areas where LS3P has devoted particular effort to reducing conflict and error. LISTENING: frequently, firms ignore the stated or implied needs and desires of their clients. SERVICE: too often, professionals forget who the client is and who is paying the bills. Our vision statement, *Solutions through Listening, Service by Design*, sets the standard by which LS3P practices.

Our client is a most significant part of the design team, being a key player in programming, through final inspection, occupancy, and maintenance. The client is integral to the process from identification of the problem through the development of the solution. A great source of pride at LS3P is that not only does the client often feel he has played a significant role in total project delivery, he actually has.

A sense of community and involvement has, from the first days, played a major role in the philosophy of the business and professional success of the firm. Playing leading and supporting roles in issues firmly believed to be in the public's best interest, and serving on civic and professional boards and committees, leaders of the firm have long committed their knowledge and resources to create a better environ. Six members of the firm have been AIA Chapter Presidents. We have led chambers of commerce, a professional licensing board, civic and professional foundations, and participated in, and chaired, design juries. Thom Penney is the 2003 President of the American Institute of Architects. We believe in being involved, in giving back.

LS3P architecture addresses the project's place, location, and context. Whether a project is urban, isolated, being rebuilt, adapted, or restored, it must belong to its environment, its location, its purpose. The many design awards received by the Charleston office or the Charlotte group attest to the absolute commitment of the entire staff to quality, attention to detail, and professionalism. Phillips Place in Charlotte is perhaps one of the more significant examples of LS3P's careful blending of vehicular and pedestrian traffic, openness, formality, economy, careful composition and commerce.

Whether we go through the arrival and processing experience of Marine recruits at Paris Island, as Vito Pascullis did, in order to better feel and know the program, or work along with preschoolers and primary students to build a playhouse, as Susan Baker did, we involve ourselves to understand. Whether standing at the rear of a just completed place of worship and hearing the Minister whisper, 'I think we've got ourselves a church', as Frank Lucas did, or building a solar system into a school's terrazzo floor, like Thom Penney did, or negotiating a tactile maze to understand how children get in touch with their feelings in the design of a children's museum, like Mike Tribble did, the result is the same. Good design is a gift, a gift of pride, a gift for all to enjoy. Truly a gift to build on.

Gaillard Municipal
Auditorium and
Exhibition Hall

1st AIA Design Award

Blue Cross Blue Shield

1963

1965

1967

1969

1964

Lucas and Stubbs
Associates Ltd. is
formed

Firm wins Auditorium
design competition

1966

Firm staff reaches 15

1968

Poplin Engineers (MEP)
merged into firm

Frank Lucas, AIA
Architect
Frank Lucas opens
doors on one-man
office

Bordeleau Apartments

Hollings and Hawk
Law Offices

6

Vito Pascullis
joins firm

Deas Hall, The Citadel

Firm renamed Lucas &
Stubbs Associates

Thom Penney joins firm

Fort Moultrie Visitors'
Center

Beaufort Post Office

nk E. Lucas elected
sident of South
olina AIA

Frank E. Lucas AIA
chairs SC Architectural
Examiners

1970   1971   1972   1973   1974   1975   1976

Firm expands to 35

Grace Church

American Mutual Fire
Insurance Company

**LS
&L**

Firm renamed Lucas,
Stubbs and Long
Associates

Richard Powell
joins firm

Fort Stewart, Georgia
Bachelor Officers
Quarters

Stratford High School

The Penney House

Commissioners of
Public Works
Administrative Offices

10th Award for Design
Excellence

Frank Lucas elevated
AIA Fellowship

1977   1979   1981   1983

1978   **1980**   1982

Firm organized into
studios

Listed in Healthcare
Top 100 Design Firms

Vito Pascullis, Richard
Powell, and Thom
Penney become
partners in the firm,
renamed Lucas,
Stubbs, Pascullis,
Powell and Penney, Ltd.

Kings Bay Enlisted
Dining Facility

College of Charleston
Center for the Arts

Charleston
International Airport

Fire Station 16

...ntee Cooper
...adquarters

Allendale Fairfax
High School

Charleston Trident
Chamber of Commerce

Conway Riverwalk

Frank Lucas elected
Chairman and Thom
Penney elected
President of firm

1985   **1987**   **1989**

...984   **1986**   **1988**   **1990**

...n featured for '20
...rs of Design
...ellence,' Gibbs
...seum of Art

25th Award of Design
Excellence

Firm receives first
Energy Award given by
the state of South
Carolina

Thom Penney elected
to AIA Fellowship

Firm reaches staff of 50

Riverbanks Zoo

...CHITECTS

...w logo introduced

Firm receives Elizabeth
O'Neill Verner
Governor's award for
the Arts, SC Arts
Commission

Fort Bragg JFK Special
Warfare Center

Coosaw Country Club

Southend Brewery

Saks Majestic Square

Mitchell School

Charleston Office

Thom Penney President of
South Carolina AIA

MUSC Storm Eye Institute

TBA² begins a 10 year plan
for the mixed-use Morrocroft
development

Firm reaches staff of 75

1991

1993

1995

1992

1994

1996

75th Award for Design
Excellence

Tamassee Salem
Middle/High School

50th Award for Design
Excellence

Phillips Place

Country Club of Charleston

Naval Air Station Pensacola

TBA² formed

New logo designed

10

50th Piggly Wiggly Market Center

Vito Pascullis, AIA retires, and Susan Baker, AIA becomes Chief Operations Officer

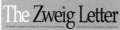

September 11, 2000: *The Zweig Letter* ranked LS3P 37 of 50 Hot Firms for 2000

Chris Ions and Jim Williams become shareholders

Barbara Price elected President of South Carolina AIA

The Zweig Letter ranked LS3P 26 of 50 Hot Firms for 2001

Cannon Street Medical Office Building

Design study for 101 South College

Charlotte/Douglas International Airport Concourse D & E

Thom Penney First Vice President/President Elect of AIA National

Crestar Riverview Center

TBA² of Charlotte, NC, merges into LS3P. Mike Tribble becomes Vice Chairman and Managing Principal of LS3P Charlotte

1997

1999

2001

1998

LS3P reaches staff of 100

nk Lucas receives South olina AIA Medal of tinction

Thom Penney named AIA National Regional Director

Tom Hund elected President of South Carolina AIA

Susan Baker along with Eric Aichele, Roger Attanasio, Richard Bartlett, Byron Edwards, Jeff Floyd, Tom Hund, Sandy Logan and John Mack are elected to shareholders

100th Award for Design Excellence

2000

April 10, 2000: *Engineering News Record* Top 500 Design A&E Firms for 1999 ranked the firm 326 and 30 among Architect firms alone

Mike Tribble elected to AIA Fellowship

Engineering News Record Top 500 Design A&E Firms for 2000 ranked the firm 26 among Architect firms alone

Warren Pruitt and George Temple become shareholders

Firm reaches staff of 184

July 2001 *Building Design & Construction* ranked the firm 28th in nation

2002

Tom Hund becomes Principal-In-Charge of the Charleston Office. Barbara Price becomes Principal-In-Charge of the Charlotte office

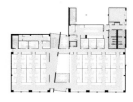

205 King Street, future home of LS3P Charleston

CHARLESTON

CHARLOTTE

New logo of merged firms

CIVIC

Charleston County Health Complex Parking Garage

Charlotte/Douglas International Airport Concourse D and E and Parking Deck

Cornelius Branch Library

Independence Regional Library

Lancaster City Hall

North Charleston Convention Center and Performing Arts Center

South Carolina Aquarium Parking Garage

1

2

1   Façade at northwest corner
2   Entry façade
3   Stair detail
4   Southeast corner showing glass elevator tower
Images: Gordon H. Schenck, Jr. Photography

Design/Completion 1992/1993
Charleston, South Carolina
Charleston County
575,000 square feet
Cast-in-place concrete, post-tensioned, pile supported, precast concrete
cladding

Charleston County Health Complex
Parking Garage

This 1,625-car parking garage, with a two-story EMS station built into the east corner of its eight and one-half level structure, derives its geometry from maximizing a triangular site at the perimeter of a regional medical center. The immediate context of this project is the western edge of a vast and largely randomly planned medical complex. The larger context of the project is the prominent architectural history of the downtown area. Responding to this larger issue places an imposing burden on a structure as utilitarian as a parking deck.

The city's most typical historic buildings have a largely vertical proportion and thus the unrelenting horizontality of a typical deck had somehow to be transferred to a more vertical sense. The precast pilasters and the frequent indentations in the exterior attempt to break the large mass into more manageable sections that can relate more directly to the desired vertical proportion. Various other details, such as precast cornice and rusticated base, metal roofs, shutters and round columns similarly demonstrate the relationship of the old city's detail. The resultant structure, then, as one drives over the western bridges into the city, introduces the visitor to the rich texture of the historic peninsula by way of a sympathetic representative of its new architectural responses to the city's storied inventory of fine 18th and 19th-century buildings.

3

4

1

1　Concourse E transition node
2　Concourse E metro-jet hub
Images: Carolina Photo Group (1); The Wilson Group (2)

Design/Completion 1999/2002
Charlotte, North Carolina
City of Charlotte Aviation Department
Concourses D and E: 400,000 square feet
Parking Deck: 375 square feet per car, two connected decks of 2,500 cars each
Concourses D and E: structural steel with exposed trusses, curved curtain-wall façades, curved standing seam roofing, interior exposed structure
Parking Deck: cast-in-place concrete, curved perforated metal panels, curtain wall at elevator and stair towers
Additional Credit: The Wilson Group (Design Architect)

Charlotte/Douglas International Airport Concourse D and E and Parking Deck

In association with The Wilson Group, LS3P ASSOCIATES LTD. is providing master planning, terminal, concourse and parking-deck design, baggage handling, and infrastructure improvements to maximize the current C/DIA complex for domestic and international travel. The team has provided master planning for Charlotte/ Douglas to provide 14,000 new in-field parking spaces, a second terminal, and concourse expansion totalling 50 new short-haul and 25 international gates. Apron taxiways, and concourse layouts, are configured to allow efficient one-way circulation at the new concourses.

Completed in 2002, the Concourse D expansion and new Concourse E greatly expand gate capacity at C/DIA. Concourse D provides four gates for long-haul international flights and seven gates for domestic or international travel, as well as expansion of the Federal Inspection Services (FIS), including Immigration and Naturalization Service (INS), Agriculture and Customs, to accommodate 1,200 passengers per hour. The new Concourse E provides 26 new commuter gates for a mix of turbo prop and regional jets, with planned expansion of an additional 11 gates.

The new parking deck will provide 5,000 spaces, and is configured to interface with an automated people mover system (APM) that will interconnect the terminal, parking decks, and a future consolidated rental car facility.

2

3 End of Concourse D showing viewing window to
  downtown Charlotte
4 Concourse E section through departure lounge
5 Decorative surroundings at helix ramps on
  parking deck
6 Concourse E circulation hub with compass
  rose floor design
Images: The Wilson Group (3–5); Carolina Photo
Group (6)

3

4

5

6

7

8

9

7   Concourse E commuter holding area
8   Perforated metal screens, featuring dramatic
     lighting effects on parking deck
9   Pedestrian courtyard at parking deck
Images: Carolina Photo Group (7); The Wilson Group
(8,9)

Design/Completion 1997/2000
Cornelius, North Carolina
Public Library of Charlotte and Mecklenburg County
5,570 square feet
Wood frame, brick veneer, wood construction, copper roofs at pavilions

Cornelius Branch Library

The facility is a 5,570 square-foot branch library located in Cornelius, North Carolina, a small town 15 miles north of Charlotte, North Carolina. Located at the corner of Catawba Avenue and Washam Road, the building is a five-minute walk from the town center. Cornelius is one of three neighboring towns (the others are Huntersville and Davidson) that have adopted neo-traditional design codes encouraging new development to occur in a way more respectful of the existing town fabric.

As you approach the town center, after exiting from I-77, you encounter several churches and a school, each of which occur in an almost deliberate rhythmic fashion along Catawba Avenue.

The challenge this project posed to the designer was to create a civic building that was harmonious in scale with surrounding residential and religious buildings, and at the same time, clearly identified itself as The Town Library. A requirement of the Town of Cornelius was that the building address the street. An entrance pavilion was created that responded to the corner and provided convenient access from the car park.

The public functions of the library are all contained within one large space with exposed structure. Large windows with window seats have been provided along Catawba Avenue. A multi-purpose reading and community room has been provided directly adjacent to the circulation room.

One of the most special features of this building is the garden pavilion. Echoing the form of the entrance pavilion, the garden pavilion provides a unique reading and escape opportunity. It has also been placed in a manner to allow children from the neighboring elementary school to visit the space with their teachers for story time.

1   Primary view of building from corner of
    Catawba Avenue and Washam Road
2   Floor plan
Images: Tim Buchman (1); LS3P ASSOCIATES LTD. (2)

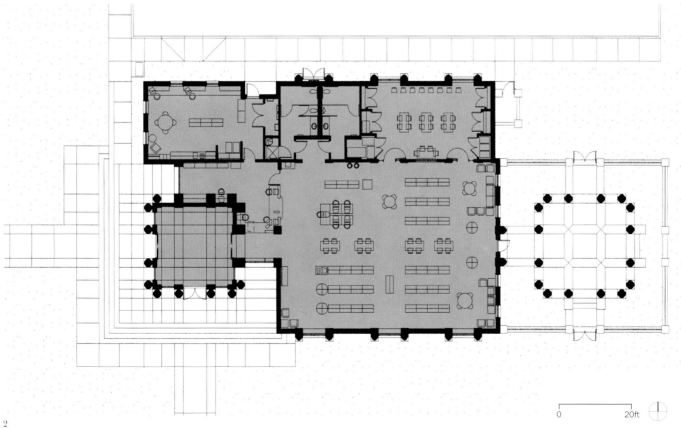

2

0   20ft

3 Garden reading pavilion
4 Interior view of main circulation space
5 Washam Road elevation looking toward entrance pavilion
Images: Tim Buchman

3

4

5

Design/Completion 1994/1996
Charlotte, North Carolina
Public Library of Charlotte and Mecklenburg County
17,300 square feet
Steel frame, load-bearing masonry, masonry, acrylic stucco, standing seam metal roof

Independence Regional Library

In 1994, the Public Library of Charlotte and Mecklenburg County commissioned LS3P ASSOCIATES LTD. to design a regional library to serve the eastern part of the city. The library selected a site near the city's major east thoroughfare. On this site was an existing single-story office building that housed the district administrative offices of a religious denomination. The building committee decided to convert the office building into the regional library.

The existing building was L-shaped in configuration. The long leg of the 'L' housed perimeter offices with core functions and internal storage. The short leg housed a meeting room, bookstore and receiving/distribution. LS3P ASSOCIATES LTD. designed the main collections and reading rooms in the original office wing. The reading room was designed as three

chambers located in the center of the wing. These chambers were designed in an enfilade fashion, each opening into the other along a central axis. Each chamber had a central skylight to provide natural light. Openings were punched into the existing load-bearing side walls, providing access to the stack areas located where the original perimeter offices had been.

Along the short leg of the 'L', LS3P ASSOCIATES LTD. located the community room, circulation desk, popular library and children's library. These spaces opened onto a new central gallery that provided access to the main collection wing. This gallery was a taller space with clerestory windows and open steel trusses. Public art lined the exterior wall of the gallery between windows. The art, in glazed brick, recalled antique frescoes with its depiction of a garden scene with plants and animals native to the Charlotte area. At the crossing of the axis of the gallery and the axis formed by the main collection reading room was the reference desk.

At the other terminus of the gallery axis was a new rotunda space. This rotunda served as entry pavilion and gave this low building a sense of civic importance.

Opposite:
Rotunda pavilion with pergola at entrance
2   Public access computer stations in children's library
Images: Michael Harrison (opposite); Joe Ciarlante (2)

2

3 Reference desk in main gallery with reading room
   for main collection beyond
4 Children's storytime area
5 Circulation desk in main gallery
Following pages:
   View of project showing rotunda pavilion, main
   gallery and main collection wing of building
Images: Joe Ciarlante (3); Joann Sieburg-Baker
(4,5, following pages)

4

3

Design/Completion 1996/1999
Lancaster, South Carolina
City of Lancaster, South Carolina
12,000 square feet
Steel frame, brick, cast stone

Lancaster City Hall

Lancaster City Hall has been constructed in the heart of a newly revitalized downtown. The building houses administrative offices, a 75-seat council chamber and the financial and utility billing departments. This City Hall incorporated the shell of an existing 4,000 square-foot bank branch, circa 1962, which had been used as the city offices for several years. A new addition totaling 8,000 square feet was added and the existing building wrapped and completely renovated in a classical style, complete with a cupola and pergola. The total effect is a building with strong civic appeal. The cupola is directly over an octagonal lobby space that acts as a focal point for the building as well as a pre-function space for the chamber. The interior is classically organized and detailed with chair rail and wainscot moldings. Ceilings of passageways are vaulted, relating directly to the arched openings leading to the spaces. Ceilings of the grand spaces are coffered and accented with crown molding. The floor of the lobby is finished in imported Italian marble slabs cut in a radial pattern.

3

Opposite:
    View of the grand hall
2   View of main lobby looking toward reception niche
3   View of main entrance of building with the pergola
    concealing a drive-thru window
Images: Tim Buchman

2

1

1　Main entrance to Performing Arts Center showing
　stage house beyond with outdoor break area
　between
2　Convention Center ballroom pre-function area
Images: Rick Alexander & Associates, Inc.

Design/Completion 1996/2000
North Charleston, South Carolina
City of North Charleston, South Carolina
Convention Center: 200,000 square feet
Performing Arts Center: 53,000 square feet
Steel frame, concrete-filled masonry, brick, stucco and metal panels

North Charleston Convention Center and Performing Arts Center

The North Charleston Convention Center houses 200,000 square feet of exhibition, banquet and meeting facilities. It is a focal point to the regional complex that includes an existing coliseum, a new performing arts center and a new hotel. The state-of-the-art facility was designed for accommodating simultaneous functions with groups of varied sizes.

Featured spaces include a 23,500 square-foot divisible ballroom with full food-preparation capabilities, a 77,000 square-foot divisible exhibition hall, and thirteen meeting rooms. Given the large-scale spaces, the design team's biggest challenge was to provide the necessary interest in detail to create a comfortable environment. Following the client's desire for the design to reference local Lowcountry themes while not imitating historical architectural styles of nearby Charleston, abstracted organic patterns common to regional nature were used to give the interior spaces a 'sense of place.'

The adjacent North Charleston Performing Arts Center is the area's largest entertainment and convention complex. The center is a facility for a variety of entertainment and community events. Its 2,300-seat auditorium, stage with elevating orchestra pit, 65-foot high fly gallery and support spaces are capable of accommodating first-rate productions and are the settings for events ranging from musicals and symphonic performances to community meetings. The design of the Performing Arts Center incorporates the use of natural 'Lowcountry' references and materials established in the connecting convention center.

2

3   Performing Arts Center auditorium
4   Performing Arts Center auditorium seating
5   Pre-function area of Performing Arts Center
Following pages:
    View of main entrance to Convention Center
    showing enclosed link to coliseum
Images: Rick Alexander & Associates, Inc.

3

4

7

7   Northwest corner of Convention Center
Opposite:
    Convention Center grand lobby entrance
Images: Rick Alexander & Associates, Inc.

1   Entry/exit elevation at night
2   Night view of corner glass stair tower
3   Detail of entry/exit bays
Images: Rick Alexander & Associates, Inc.

Design/Completion 1996/2000
Charleston, South Carolina
City of Charleston and South Carolina Electric & Gas
The Keenan Company
315,000 square feet
Precast concrete, supported on ninety-foot pre-stressed concrete driven piles, cast-in-place pile caps and grade beams, precast concrete panels with all exposed metal of stainless steel

South Carolina Aquarium Parking Garage

This parking deck provides 1,102 parking spaces for the aquarium, the National Park Service tour boat facility, an outdoor sports complex, a future maritime museum and new city symphony hall. The parking structure mediates between the office building on one side and the aquarium on the other while incorporating subtle recognition of Charleston's built heritage and the vocabulary of maritime industrial buildings.

Since the design of both the flanking buildings are so forceful, the deck design complements rather than competes, picking up aspects of both the precast and glass office building and the cast concrete, highly sculptural aquarium. The all-glass office building and the aquarium enhance the rather severe main façade. One of the more playful aspects of this design is the wave pattern cast into the panels framing the entry bay, a reference to the aquarium's logo. At night the stair towers become icons for the complex and make it highly locatable from a distance.

This is a three-bay garage, with the center bay being the two-way ramp, and the external bays flat for more uniform architectural expression. The project was awarded the Precast/Prestressed Concrete National Awards Program Special Recognition.

2

3

4   Entry/exit canopy detail
5   Corner stair detail
Images: Rick Alexander & Associates, Inc.

4

5

EDUCATION

Aiken Technical College Dale Phelon Information Technology Center

Allendale Fairfax High School

Battery Creek High School

Lake City Primary School

Porter Gaud School Science and Technology Center

Saluda Trail Middle School

University of North Carolina at Charlotte Engineering Research Building

Washington and Lee University School of Journalism

Design/Completion 1997/2000
Aiken, South Carolina
Aiken Technical College
40,000 square feet
Steel frame, brick veneer, metal roofing,
aluminum storefront and grilles, glass block

Aiken Technical College Dale Phelon
Information Technology Center

The Information Technology Center at
Aiken Technical College consolidates a
new college library and computer
laboratories in one building, centrally
located on the campus. The building
includes a two-story L-shaped classroom
component, with the library occupying a
curved area between the two wings. The
rounded form of the library responds to a
turn in the campus master plan and allows
all shelving to be laid out on a radial layout
for easy supervision of the library. The
exterior reinforces a campus vocabulary
of two brick sizes and colors along with
accents of metal roofing.

2

3

1&3   Entry-stair tower
  2   Library
Images: Rick Alexander & Associates, Inc.

1

2

Design/Completion 1984/1987
Allendale, South Carolina
Allendale County School Board
118,000 square feet
Steel frame with precast concrete and masonry

Allendale Fairfax High School

Designed as the core for a 900-student facility, this addition adjoins an existing vocational building to form a comprehensive new high school. The cafeteria and a skylit commons are used to form a link between the existing school and a new classroom wing. The stepped form of the commons expresses itself as a triangular canopy at the public entry, providing a strong statement of entrance to a necessarily long façade of old and new construction. The commons serves as a focal point for the school as well as a lobby for the gymnasium and cafeteria. The classroom wing is treated similarly to the existing building to provide a balanced façade and to further emphasize the entry.

1   Media center
2   Exterior view of entrance
3   Interior view of commons
Images: Brian Dressler

3

1

2

1 View of front façade
2 Exterior view of stairwell
3 View from playing fields
Images: Rick Alexander & Associates, Inc.

Design/Completion 1990/1992
Beaufort County, South Carolina
Beaufort County Schools
220,000 square feet
Steel frame, brick and split-faced concrete block

Battery Creek High School

The facility is a new 220,000 square-foot school for 1,500 students with a 1,000-seat auditorium, 1,500-seat gymnasium, music and art rooms, vocational facilities, media center, cafeteria, and administrative and guidance offices. Site development includes parking, playing fields, retention ponds and stadium.

The building is organized around the concept of an educational mall which runs from the front public entry to the rear student entry. This central circulation spine extends out into the site as an organizational element for the parking lot and athletic fields. The common and community-use spaces are located off this mall. The second floor consists of general-purpose classrooms that are repetitive in layout, removed from the noise and activity of the ground floor. The exterior of the building utilizes traditional 'school house red' brick and split-faced concrete block in classical, formal design to create a sense of history, style and permanence.

3

4

5

4   View of front portico
5   Interior view of cafeteria
Opposite:
    Interior view of gymnasium
Images: Rick Alexander & Associates, Inc.

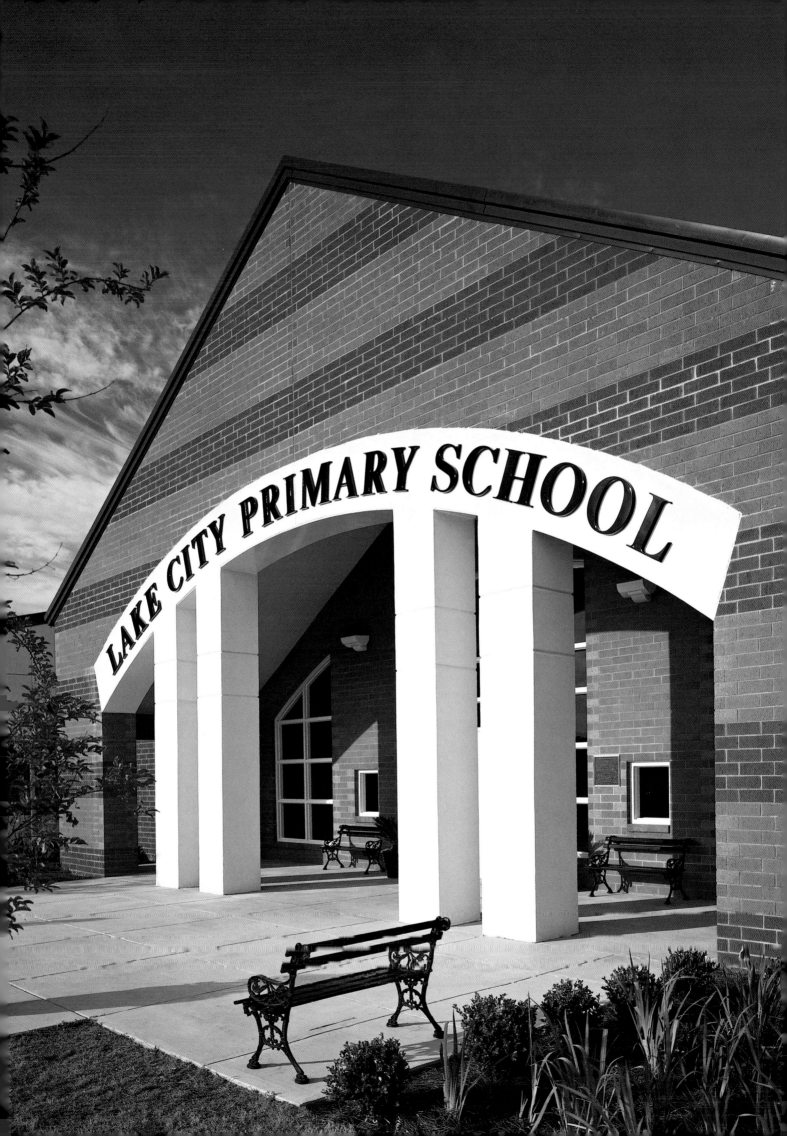

Design/Completion 1994/1996
Lake City, South Carolina
Florence County School District 3
66,000 square feet
Load-bearing CMU with pre-engineered metal roof system, brick veneer, stucco over concrete block,
pre-engineered metal roof system

Lake City Primary School

The four wings or 'houses' which comprise this primary school facility are arranged around a central outdoor courtyard, which provides a secure outdoor area for use by these young students without distractions from the adjacent high school. The alignment of the houses with the directions on a compass provides a subtle learning opportunity for students, by means of a 'rising sun' window in the yellow east house, a red 'setting sun' louver in the west house and a compass and 'north star' in the courtyard.

This facility is 66,000 square feet and was designed for 800 students. Features include general purpose, resource, and special purpose classrooms, art, music, and PE rooms, media center, administrative and guidance offices, and a cafeteria with stage, kitchen and central receiving. Special attention was paid to the details throughout to help all of the children feel at home in this building. Examples of such details include a miniature bank, post office and school store spaces for operation by the students, and a small-scale entrance door and 'fireplace' backdrop for the reading area in the media center to support an emphasis on reading.

Opposite:
   Entry porch
2   View of 'rising sun' window
3   View of 'setting sun' and compass in courtyard
Images: Rick Alexander & Associates, Inc.

6

5

1 Technology center
5 Media center with 'fireplace' and 'rising sun' window
6 Lobby
Images: Rick Alexander & Associates, Inc.

1

2

Design/Completion 1996/1999
Charleston, South Carolina
Porter Gaud School
39,350 square feet
Steel frame and load-bearing masonry, brick veneer, precast concrete trim, standing seam metal
roofing, terrazzo flooring

Porter Gaud School Science and Technology Center

1 View of front and main entry
2 View from campus green
3 New campus entry gates with facility in background
4 Library
Images: Rick Alexander & Associates, Inc.

Porter Gaud is a private kindergarten-through-12th grade school with a distinguished record for graduating highly-motivated college-bound students. This addition to the campus was part of a master plan to update and expand the campus for the new millennium. One of the principal objectives of the master plan was to create, in concert with the reorganization of the entrance sequence and circulation, a new focus for the center of the campus. The majority of the existing buildings were an undistinguished assembly of structures built during the 1950s and 1960s for its original campus, and the school possessed neither a sense of arrival nor any hint of the long history of the institution. The task of the building was, then, to create this missing center and at the same time allude to traditional architectural expressions of older educational institutions.

It was decided to abstract older buildings from typical educational models since the existing campus has no such iconography. The design of the new building loosely uses the Palladian compositional elements of central mass attached to flankers with abbreviated colonnaded connectors. The principal mass is punctuated by a two-story porch that alludes to the building's role as school center and the lobby continues through to actualize its role as 'gateway' to the interior campus. The building includes campus administrative offices, a library, computer labs and science labs for grades Seven to twelve.

3

4

Design/Completion 1996/1999
Rock Hill, South Carolina
Rock Hill School District 3
160,000 square feet
Steel frame and load-bearing masonry, brick, metal panels

Saluda Trail Middle School

The overall layout of this project, for grades six through eight, responds to the topography of the site, thus locating the buildings and athletic fields in a gentle arc along the existing ridge line. The floor plan design for the facility represents the educational goals and curriculum of the district, organized around a multipurpose gallery space. The three-dimensional built forms and image are derived from cues found in the urban parts of Rock Hill,

as represented by the 'village' side of the gallery, and the more rural or residential areas of Rock Hill, as represented by the 'house' side of the gallery.

The facility includes 160,000 square feet and is designed for 1,000 students (infrastructure for 1,200) with general and special-purpose classrooms, computer labs, media center, gymnasium with regulation-size basketball court, 500-seat auditorium, industrial and home art rooms, choral, band and orchestra rooms, kitchen and cafeteria, and administrative and guidance offices. The site program includes a football field with track and field house, soccer and softball fields, and tennis and basketball courts.

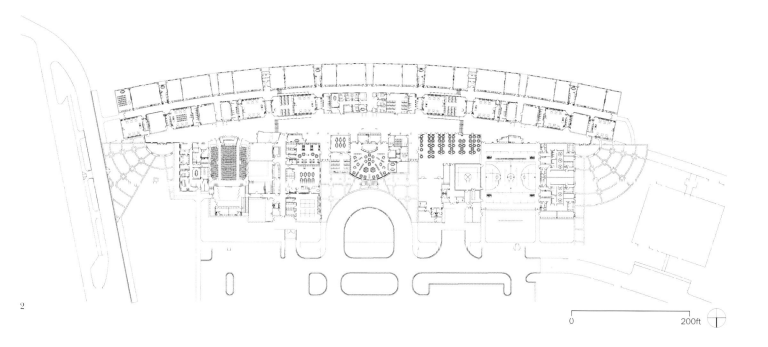

2

0   200ft

1   Bus canopy
2   Floor plan
Images: Rick Alexander & Associates, Inc. (1);
LS3P ASSOCIATES LTD. (2)

3   Pedestrian spine to athletic fields
4   Gallery: gymnasium entrance
5   Gallery: 'house' and auditorium entrance
Images: Rick Alexander & Associates, Inc.

3

4

5

7

6

6   Gallery and media center 'house' entrances
7   Gallery, exploratory area
Opposite:
    Entry canopy
Images: Rick Alexander & Associates, Inc.

1

2

Design/Completion 2001/2004
Charlotte, North Carolina
University of North Carolina at Charlotte
112,000 square feet
Concrete frame, brick, cast stone, metal roof, Low-E glass
Additional Credit: ColeJenset & Stone (Master Planning)

University of North Carolina at Charlotte Engineering Research Building

The Engineering Research Building is one of the first two buildings to be built at the gateway of the new Charlotte Institute of Technology Innovation Campus at the University of North Carolina at Charlotte. The 112,000 square-foot classroom and office building will support the vernacular of the classical themes that have adorned the most prestigious institutes of higher education in America. Motor sports engineering, the Center for Precision Design and Metrology, mechanical engineering, thermal/bio-engineering and other technology-rich curricula will occupy the facility. The campus is oriented around an elliptical green and the Engineering Research Building occupies a prominent location on the green. The building is designed in a Tuscan order with an entrance portico and terrace. The interior of the building is classically organized with a two-story colonnade surrounding an elliptical lobby.

Sustainability and Green Architecture are hallmarks of the building's design, with the use of partly recycled materials such as steel, aluminum, glass, and asphalt. The northeast to southwest orientation of the building, and the natural fall of the site, have been utilized to minimize solar heat gain and maximize efficiency of the heating, ventilating and air-conditioning systems. The Center for Precision Design and Metrology, with its vibration-and-light-sensitive laboratories, is built into the hillside, to maximize insulation and isolation.

Insulated low-E glazing is used throughout, with electronically-controlled lighting using multiple and zonal settings.

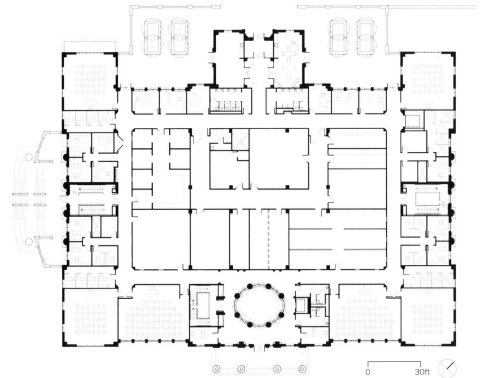

3

4

1 View from the 'ellipse' toward the main entrance
2 View from the green toward the alternate entrance
3 Second-floor plan
4 View from the circle at the new campus entrance
Images: LS3P ASSOCIATES LTD.

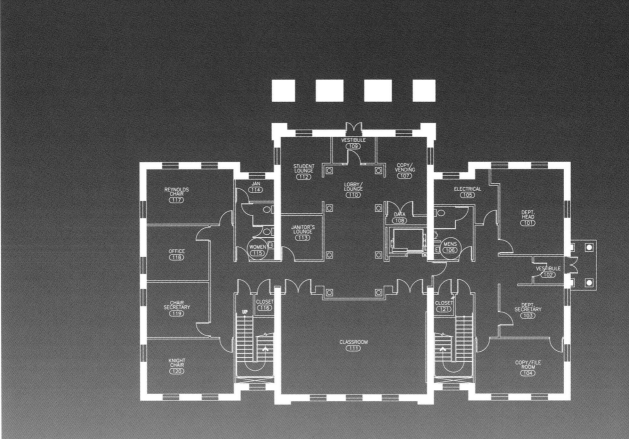

FIRST FLOOR PLAN

SOUTHEAST ELEVATION

Design/Completion 2000/August 2002
Lexington, Virginia
Washington and Lee University
17,500 square feet
Load-bearing masonry exterior, new steel framed interior, double-hung windows,
copper standing seam roofing

Washington and Lee University
School of Journalism, Reid Hall

Designed in 1908 by famed St. Louis architect Theo C. Link, Reid Hall occupies a site on the promenade of the historic Washington and Lee campus. To prepare the School of Journalism for the digital transformation of broadcast news, a complete new building interior was provided with new steel framing, new mechanical and electrical systems, and classroom, seminar, broadcast studio, and editing spaces. These are configured for current teaching practices, and supported by a new digital media spine. The historic building exterior was faithfully restored consistent with Theo Link's original drawings.

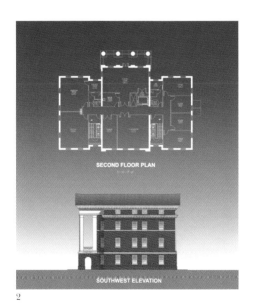

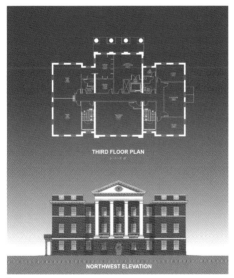

2

3

4

1 First-floor plan, southeast elevation
2 Second-floor plan, southwest elevation
3 Third-floor plan, northwest elevation
4 Fourth-floor plan, northeast elevation
Images: LS3P ASSOCIATES LTD.

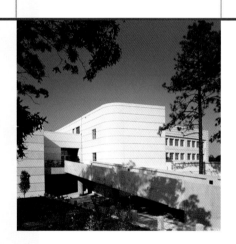

FEDERAL

Fort Bragg JFK Special Warfare Center

Fort Jackson US Army Soldier Support Institute

Naval Air Station Pensacola Barracks, Dining and Recreation Complex

1

1　View of ceremonial entrance, administrative offices
　　and stepped lecture hall
2　View of ceremonial lobby
3　View of pedestrian bridge between administrative
　　offices and academic wing
Images: Gordon H. Schenck, Jr. Photography

Design/Completion 1985/1992
Fayetteville, North Carolina
United States Army Corps of Engineers,
Savannah District
186,000 square feet
Concrete frame, precast concrete

Fort Bragg JFK Special Warfare Center

This military academic facility includes language laboratories, computer-aided instruction spaces, and training areas for special subjects. The program has led to a form consisting of three blocks, two providing instructional spaces, and the third housing the library and office areas.

The challenge of a steeply-sloping site was addressed by the incorporation of three ramps located at circulation nodal points, allowing students to proceed from the parking area to both classroom levels without the use of stairs.

The ceremonial entrance, accentuated by a large shield-like form, faces the major thoroughfare, while the angled extension containing the library gestures toward the neighboring group of buildings. Like the military branch it serves, the facility projects an image of quiet strength and solidity.

The positioning of the building, down the slope and slightly away from the parking level, created a buffer area where existing trees and other vegetation was protected during construction. Truck access on the lowest level from the back of the classroom block was also made possible by the positioning of the building down the slope. This facility stands apart from the neighboring groups of buildings, in the same manner as the special forces who conduct their training here, stand apart from the rest of the military forces.

2

3

Design/Completion 1991/1994
Columbia, South Carolina
US Army Corps of Engineers, Savannah District
240,000 square feet
Steel frame, brick veneer with concrete masonry back-up

Fort Jackson US Army Soldier Support Institute

The United States Army Soldier Support Institute is a 240,000 square-foot complex with classrooms for three training schools, library, 250-seat auditorium, snack bar, exchange facility and offices for 400 instructional staff. Located on the highest point of the post, Tank Hill, the structure is organized by a stucco spine running the 500-foot length of the site from the ceremonial entrance canopy opposite the post's water tank, to the auditorium and exchange. The three-story spine is level with the school structures that project 'down' the hill and parallels the office block located a half-level 'up' the hill.

The corridor running the length of the spine has alternating stairs and vending areas with views down the hill and across the post. The impact of the long office block is minimized with projecting concrete masonry bays that align with the schools and allude to the rotated tower entrances that terminate the school structures. The wall of the auditorium structure is battered to recall the many fort structures that populate South Carolina historical sites. Split-faced concrete masonry is stepped a quarter inch per course and is capped by a precast coping and railing, projected out towards the top like the apparatus of so many army vehicles populating the Fort Jackson landscape.

Opposite:
West end of spine at auditorium
2 View from southwest showing spine extending out from brick 'schoolhouse' and past fortress-inspired auditorium
Images: Gordon H. Schenck, Jr. Photography

2

3 View up Tank Hill to three schools and spine
4 View from southeast to three school entrances
5 Interior view along spine between school structures
Images: Gordon H. Schenck, Jr. Photography

3

4

5

1

1   E1-E4 barracks with stair tower and study rooms in
    foreground. Entrance plaza beyond
2   Barracks grouped to form courtyard spaces for
    student off-duty activity
3   Aerial photo of entire complex with Pensacola Bay
    in foreground
Images: Rick Alexander & Associates, Inc. (1,2);
ASA Photo-Graphics/Al Audelman (3)

Design/Completion 1993/1995
Pensacola, Florida
Southern Division Naval Facilities Engineering Command (NAVFAC)
Over 1.4 million square feet
Cast-in-place concrete and structural steel framing, non load-bearing metal studs with brick veneer and acrylic stucco

Naval Air Station Pensacola Barracks, Dining and Recreation Complex

As part of the early 1990s Base Realignment and Closure Commission directives, the navy was required to relocate the Naval Air Technical Training Center to NAS Pensacola. Southern Division NAVFAC was faced with acquiring design services for a fully-functional, self-sufficient training complex, to be located on an abandoned air field at the southeast end of the Air Station. This complex was to house, feed, educate, and train 5,000 young enlisted men and women. It was also required to provide recreation, medical, and personal needs, maximizing training time during their short stay.

The results are eight three-story, 117,480 square-foot barracks buildings for enlisted ranks of E1-E4, each accommodating 560 students, for a total of 4,480 students and 939,840 square feet; one six-story barracks building for enlisted ranks of E5-E6, accommodating 444 students in 279,174 square feet; a 56,760 square-foot dining facility; a central energy plant; Morale Welfare Recreation (MWR) facilities including bowling alley, weight rooms, movie theater, auto-hobby shops and a navy exchange, in renovated historic hangar buildings; a new enlisted club; and outdoor parade grounds and ceremonial spaces for change of command and graduations.

LS3P ASSOCIATES LTD. received the Navy Certificate of Appreciation for Exemplary Performance.

2

3

4   E1-E4 barracks entrance
5   E1-E4 courtyard for volleyball, cookout area
6   E5-E6 barracks six-story structure

Images: Rick Alexander & Associates, Inc.

4

9

8

Opposite:
   View of barracks from dining facility entrance plaza
   and outdoor dining spaces
8   Dining facility entrance canopy
9   E5-E6 barracks loggia with fire truck access to
     courtyard

Images: Rick Alexander & Associates, Inc.

10 E5-E6 barracks main entry
11 Interior of historic hanger renovated for MWR use
Images: Rick Alexander & Associates, Inc.

10

11

INTERIORS

LandDesign Studio

Ness Motley Law Office

Newton Builders Corporate Office

Pilgrim Court II Corporate Facility

Volvo Administration Facility

Wall Street Capitol Corporate Offices

Design/Completion 1999/2001
Charlotte, North Carolina
LandDesign Incorporated
22,000 square feet
Structural steel frame, brick, aluminum-clad wood windows, stained concrete flooring

LandDesign Studio

When LandDesign, a national land planning and civil engineering firm, had outgrown its existing location in Charlotte, the firm decided they wanted to relocate within the Center City in a building that reflected the more urban nature of their current practice and in a location and environment that would be appealing to both their staff and clients. The firm decided upon an urban infill site, part of the Charlotte Cotton Mills, a project they master planned. The Charlotte Cotton Mills project occupies a full city block in an old industrial district, four blocks from The Square, the center of uptown Charlotte.

The LandDesign headquarters is the first completed component of that mixed-use project that will include the renovation and reuse of the building, the city's first cotton mill, dating back to the late 1880s, and a new multi-family residential component and parking deck.

Located at the northeast corner of the block, the four-story LandDesign building incorporates the two street façades of Charlotte's original Coca-Cola bottling plant that dates from the early 1900s. The façades are all that remain of the original structure, which collapsed several years ago. The shift in the building's plan axis is derived from the original façade aligning with the site's north-south street and the new façade primarily aligning with its east-west street.

In plan, the building utilizes the existing brick firewall shared with the neighboring historic four-story building as part of a circulation gallery onto which the building's core functions open. This gallery is used as exhibition space for firm projects. Beyond the core is the column-free expanse of the major studio spaces. These studio spaces receive natural light from large north-facing operable windows. Meeting and gathering spaces are located primarily along the building's east façade with large windows facing the city's skyline and with access to a third floor terrace created by the juxtaposition of the original façade with the new façade. The headquarters are designed with a public lobby and conference center on the first floor, with the remainder of the floor available for street level retail use.

Interior finishes in the LandDesign studio include stained concrete floors, exposed brick walls, wood windows, and exposed structure and mechanical systems at the ceiling level; all to be compatible with the nearby renovated historic manufacturing spaces. As a visual counterpoint, studio workstations and reception desks are finished in light maple veneer. Lighting levels are designed around task lighting, focused on work surfaces and accent lighting.

Opposite:
Reception desk at visitors' waiting
2   Street-level reception lobby with conference room beyond
Images: Tim Buchman

2

3

3 Studio view with open workstations along north wall
  and individual engineering work stations along core
4 Detail of maple veneer-clad workstation
5 Conference room with city view in background
Images: Tim Buchman

4

1

1   Elevator lobby
2   Fifth floor senior partner reception area
3   Main building lobby
Images: Rion Rizzo/Creative Sources

Design/Completion 1998/2000
Mt. Pleasant, South Carolina
Ness Motley
120,000 square feet
Venetian stucco, Makore wood wall panels, patterned granite floors and carpet
Additional credit: In collaboration with McKellar & Associates Architects

Ness Motley Law Office

Overlooking the tranquil marshlands along the Cooper River is the headquarters for Ness Motley, a nationally recognized law firm. Included in the 120,000 square-foot office space are the grand lobby, reception and conferencing centers, a mock court room, law library, video conferencing facility, fitness center, employee dining room, and a rooftop pavilion.

The double-story grand entrance lobby is clad with Venetian stucco and Makore wood wall panels, and patterned granite floors. The state-of-the-art moot court room and conferencing areas are fully equipped with audiovisual and teleconferencing equipment concealed within feature millwork pieces. A pull-out touch screen for operating multimedia digital presentations slides into the apron of the custom conference table when not in use. The elevator core is expressed and articulated with wood architectural panels rising through all floors of the building as a way-finding device for its occupants. To provide an upscale modular office environment, a wood and fabric furniture system with doors and indirect ambient lighting was designed for all non-partner positions. Beautifully detailed recessed file units with posting shelves line the corridors outside each partner's office, allowing individual office suites to be free of paper clutter.

2

3

5

Opposite:
    Typical reception area
5   Typical open office area
Images: Rion Rizzo/Creative Sources

Design/Completion 1996/1999
Charleston, South Carolina
Newton Builders
Piggly Wiggly Carolina Company
11,300 square feet
Swiss pearwood casework and paneling, glass and stainless steel divider, carpet

Newton Builders Corporate Office

Once an abandoned distribution warehouse center for a major food manufacturer, this adaptive re-use project is the new home for a commercial general contracting company. Due to increased growth in company personnel, the client was seeking additional space to relocate its offices, with additional room for warehouse storage. It was also looking for an opportunity to showcase its construction expertise to potential clients visiting the space. This 11,300 square-foot renovation houses offices, reception, conference, kitchen, warehouse storage and indoor parking. The contemporary design is expressed in a composition of wood, stone, steel and glass, a metaphor for the primary materials used in commercial building.

A strong grid pattern was established to unite the exterior with the interior. On the outside, the grid is expressed using metal panels and a new glass and aluminum storefront. A stainless-steel railing with a mahogany top rail leads from a cast-in-place concrete ramp and stair to the main entry, signified by a custom-steel canopy composed using structural steel shapes. On the inside, the grid carries through the interior of the public areas, using panels of Swiss pearwood, glass and stainless steel. On a glass and steel divider, denoting the entry from the main lobby, all attachments are expressed honestly using steel hex bolts, further reinforcing the 'construction' metaphor.

The reception desk also incorporates the use of wood, stone, stainless steel and glass. The organic sweep of the Swiss pearwood front provides a relief from the grid pattern surrounding it. The glass transaction surface above is supported at one end by a vertical plane of steel slicing through the black granite below. Signage was designed by laser cutting the client's logo onto two stainless steel sheets, internally illuminated from a glass panel beyond. Floating off the walls, photographs of the client's built projects are sandwiched between planes of acrylic sheets and secured at each corner with steel pins.

In the main conference room, a glass credenza cantilevers from the wall with polished stainless steel brackets. At one end, a sculptural column of reinforcing steel rises through an opening in the glass top. A light buried within its concrete base casts a dramatic shadow through the vertical and spiral members of the column. General illumination of this room was accomplished by suspended low-voltage lamps from two sets of electrically powered steel cables. A gridded carpet was chosen to further reinforce the concept.

1   Reception area toward reception desk
2   Main conference room
3   Reception area toward divider screen
Images: Rick Alexander & Associates Inc.

2

3

Design/Completion 1991/1994
Winston-Salem, North Carolina
Pilgrim Associates LLC
110,000 square feet
Composite steel and concrete frame, architectural precast, aluminum curtain wall, high-performance glazing

Pilgrim Court II Corporate Facility

This corporate facility houses data processing and management functions. The major interior entry and public corridor connects the two-story entry to the elevator lobby and the monumental stair to the garden level. This grid-patterned and paneled sequence of varied but connected volumes comprises the primary public spaces for this four-story corporate office building. The main level of the corridor sequence had to proceed completely through the building connecting the upper-level second floor conference area at one end and the lower-level training center at the other end. The establishment of a public connecting element from one side of the building to the other allowed for a variety of two-story volumes which had a source of natural light at each end.

Opposite:
Monumental stair connector from first floor to lower level training and cafeteria facilities
2   Second-floor conference room overlooking the two-story reception/lobby
Images: Tim Buchman

2

3

3   Typical corridor
4   Elevator lobby
5   Reception/waiting
Images: Tim Buchman

4

5

1

Design/Completion 1994/1998
Greensboro, North Carolina
Volvo Trucks North America, Inc.
165,000 square feet
Steel-frame, brick veneer, porcelain tile, carpet over raised floor, stained and natural maple wood paneling

Volvo Administration Facility

This two-story building was originally designed as a new product showplace on Volvo's Greensboro campus and was converted to new corporate offices, totaling 165,000 square feet. Volvo desired to maintain the established image of the existing campus with the use of natural light, wood finishes and contemporary Swedish design lines.

A primary feature of the building is the skylit galleria. This continuous spine acts as a central organizer for the building and a staff gathering place. Conference rooms, staff work areas and core-type functions occur along the spine.

The boardroom and executive offices located on the second floor utilize stained and natural maple wood paneling as accents. A grand stair provides convenient access from the main lobby to the executive suite. There is an executive lobby at the head of the stair that serves as a pre-function space for board functions. The President's office is located adjacent the boardroom to provide a separate entrance for the executive's use.

2

1   Galleria
2   Reception area adjacent board room and
     President's office
3   Main lobby
Images: Rick Alexander & Associates, Inc.

3

Design/Completion 1999/2000
Charlotte, North Carolina
Wall Street Capitol
18,500 square feet
Bubinga and Kewazingo wood panels, stone, carpet, fabric-wrapped panels, glass, polished stainless steel

Wall Street Capitol Corporate Offices

As a national network for one-stop financial shopping, Wall Street Capitol provides a full range of capital investment services to high-net-worth clients, predominately in the high-tech arena. The interior bespeaks Old World investing with clean architectural lines.

Set on axis to the entrance is a dramatic 25-foot palatial exterior window with a free-standing wood feature wall that separates

the grand lobby from the boardroom beyond. Recessed within this feature wall is a 350-gallon salt-water aquarium open to each room. Glass panels surround the feature wall and penetrate the vaulted ceiling above to allow both visual access and acoustical control. The free-standing wood feature wall required a major engineering effort to maintain tasteful and clean architectural lines. To carry the water load of the aquarium, the structural slab below was heavily reinforced. Architectural wood panels of Kewazingo were clipped to a structural steel cage that supported both the weights of the aquarium and the butt-glazed glass panels above.

1 View of main lobby with custom reception desk
2 View from elevator lobby leading to main entrance reception
Images: Rion Rizzo/Creative Sources

2

3 View of boardroom
Opposite:
  View of wood feature wall in main reception area
Images: Rion Rizzo/Creative Sources

3

MIXED USE

101 South College Street

AXA Berry Hill

Ballantyne Resort Hotel and Clubhouse

Consolidated Theatres

Fifth & Poplar Residential Complex

Kiawah Sales and Information Center

Lodge Alley Inn Renovation

Midtown Square Master Plan

Morrocroft Centre

Phillips Place Lifestyle Center

SouthPark Regional Mall

Wild Dunes Resort Grand Pavilion

Design/Completion 1999/2000
Charlotte, North Carolina
Lincoln Harris
Office: 750,000 square feet
Retail: 60,000 square feet
Residential: 80 Condominium units
Hotel: 200 rooms/suites
Parking: 1,200 spaces
Structural steel above cast concrete, granite, precast concrete, glass

101 South College Street

This master plan study is for a parcel located one block south of the Square at the very heart of Charlotte's uptown business district. The urban mixed-use development includes three main components: an office tower, a residential tower and a hotel tower all adjoined around a central plaza.

The office tower is 36 stories with 750,000 square feet, capped with two penthouse levels articulated with temple porticos.

Flanking the office tower are two mid-rise towers for the condominiums and hotel. All three buildings rise from a three-story plinth which accommodates lobby spaces, retail/restaurant spaces, the conferencing center of the hotel and large floor-plate opportunities for the office tenants.

The retail component fronts College Street, Trade Street, Third Street and the plaza. Retail also flanks two skylight galleries on either side of the office tower. These galleries connect at the rear of the block to the light rail/trolley stop for the Center City.

The tower and the plinth all sit above a four-level parking structure of 1,200 spaces beneath the College Street grade.

The plaza is the visual and pedestrian center of the project. Outdoor dining for the restaurants spills out along the perimeter arcades of the plaza. A central motor court provides drop-off access for the office and residential buildings.

At the very heart of the plaza is a monumental interactive water feature.

The architectural design of the project is evocative of the romantic architecture of the 'Age of Skyscraper'. A stylized classical language is utilized and the façades are modulated to create a strong sense of verticality to the shaft. The penthouses receive most attention as the cap of each building. The office tower is crowned with half-dormers and capped with a columned, domed lantern.

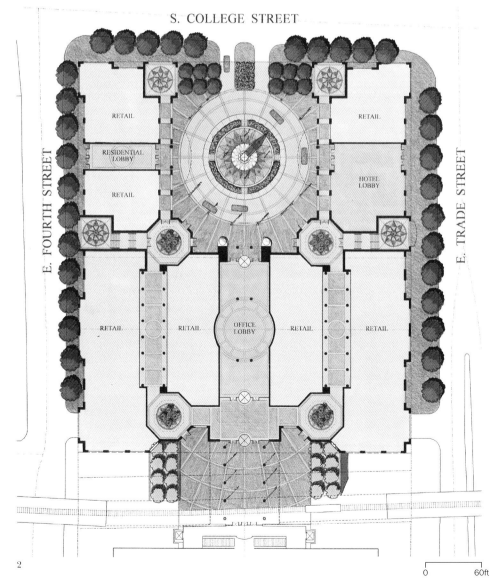

S. COLLEGE STREET

E. FOURTH STREET

E. TRADE STREET

RETAIL

RETAIL

RESIDENTIAL LOBBY

HOTEL LOBBY

RETAIL

RETAIL

RETAIL

OFFICE LOBBY

RETAIL

RETAIL

2

0   60ft

1   Rendering of mixed-use complex showing plaza along College Street
2   Public Spaces Plan showing pedestrian connections to the streets, through plaza to light rail/trolley station
Images: Risden McElroy (1); LS3P ASSOCIATES LTD. (2)

Design/Completion 1998/1999
South Boston, Virginia
The AXA Group
Existing mansion: 15,000 square feet
New additions: 91,500 square feet
Existing mansion: load bearing masonry with wood, hand-made brick, terne-coated stainless steel roof
New additions: composite steel and concrete frames, brick and standing seam roofing

AXA Berry Hill

This historic restoration centers around the mansion Berry Hill, erected in 1842-44 for James Coles Bruce. Designated a National Historic Landmark, this estate was purchased by The AXA Group, a French-based insurance and financial services company for use as a training center. The project involved a museum-quality restoration of the mansion with very discreet, architecturally compatible new wings for classrooms, dining room and offices. The project also includes traditional-style buildings to accommodate ninety guestrooms and a health spa. AXA Berry Hill is a unique conference center and corporate retreat in South Boston, Virginia, serving the AXA Group of insurance companies worldwide. It complements two existing AXA facilities in the Bordeaux region of France.

At the heart of Berry Hill is the adaptive re-use of the Greek Revival mansion for social gatherings, meetings and VIP accommodation. Additions to the mansion provided in new buildings adjacent to the historic mansion are a dining salon for 120 people and classrooms and break-out rooms for up to 72 trainees on 24,000 square feet; a 59,000 square-foot, 90-room residential hotel; and a 8,500 square foot fitness center with a 25-meter indoor pool, saunas and complete physical plant on the bottom floor.

The three-story mansion is built of hand-made brick with walls up to two feet thick. The existing metal roof was replaced with a new terne-coated stainless steel roof to stabilize the structure. The original stucco finish on the front and sides of the mansion, scored to resemble blocks of stone, was completely restored. The exposed brick on the back of the mansion and the service range was maintained. The original brick was cleaned and repointed. Original decorative plaster ceilings, marble fireplace surrounds, heart pine floors and silver plated hardware were restored. New mechanical systems were inserted into the attic and cellar of the mansion, and a new central mechanical plant provides chilled water for the entire complex.

The classroom and dining salon additions to the mansion are steel-frame construction with brick exterior, painted to match the stucco finish of the mansion. Floors in public circulation areas are slate with carpet in classrooms and break-out rooms, and heart pine in the dining salon. State-of-the-art audiovisual and telecommunication systems are provided throughout the facility, with simultaneous translation capability in English and two foreign languages for all training programs. Connections for laptop computers have been located in break-out areas and all guest rooms in the complex.

2

Opposite:
    AXA Berry Hill historic façade of existing mansion
2   Covered breezeway flanking main courtyard
Images: John Hall

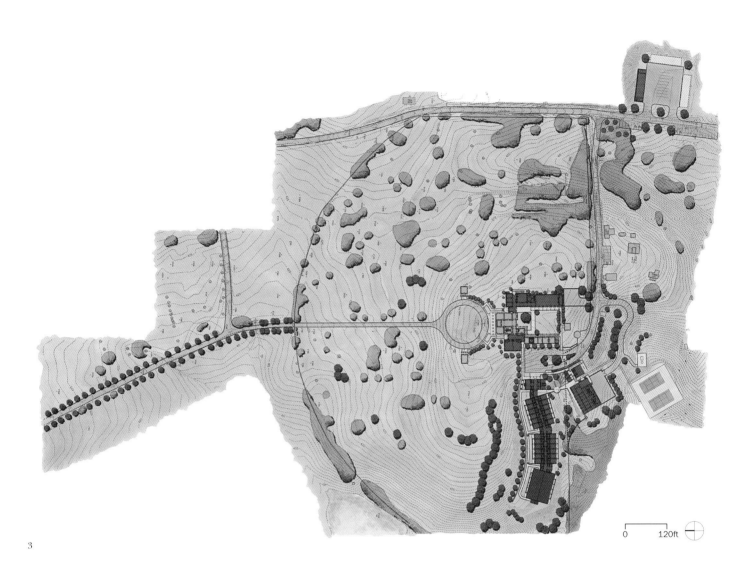

3

0   120ft

4

5

3   Site plan
4   Indoor pool
5   New dining salon addition to existing mansion
Images: John Hall (5); Rodger Hinton (4);
LS3P ASSOCIATES LTD. (3)

7

8

6   Renovated salon in mansion
7   Ancillary-use buildings from main courtyard
8   Entry drive to AXA Berry Hill training facilities
Images: John Hall

1

Design/Completion 1999/2002
Charlotte, North Carolina
The Bissell Companies
Hotel: 184,000 square feet, 216 rooms
Conference Center: 42,000 square feet
Clubhouse: 30,000 square feet
Spa: 18,000 square feet
Concrete for hotel, steel frame for other structures, stone, cast stone, acrylic stucco

Ballantyne Resort Hotel and Clubhouse

1 Central element of the entry façade with the porte-cochere and fountain at the motor court in the foreground
2 Rendering of motor court and porte-cochere
Following pages:
   Resort hotel from the lake at the 18th green
   Spa to the right of the photo. Conference center and clubhouse to the left
Images: Peter Brentlinger (1); Risden McElroy (2); Rick Alexander & Associates, Inc. (following pages)

In 1999, The Bissell Companies commissioned LS3P ASSOCIATES LTD. to master plan and design the hotel, clubhouse, conference center, golf school and spa for their 'urban resort' envisioned for the corporate business park at their 2,000-acre planned community, Ballantyne. The centerpiece of the resort is the 18-hole golf course, which runs through Ballantyne Corporate Business Park. The vision for the urban resort was to provide all of the amenities of a true resort/conference center like Pinehurst with the convenience of being within 30 minutes of Charlotte's hub airport.

The complex was built in an L-shape configuration around the 18th hole of the golf course. The first phase of the resort was the three-story clubhouse, which houses the pro-shop, locker rooms, grill room, bar and the resort's initial meeting rooms and kitchen facilities. Phase Two consisted of the 216-room full-service hotel and 42,000 square-foot conference center. Public areas of the hotel center around the two-story colonnaded main lobby and focuses panoramic views to the 18th fairway and overall course. The conference center is a two-level facility featuring a 6,500 square-foot ballroom and assorted meeting rooms organized around a main gallery within a grand monumental stair overlooking the 18th green. Phase Three, completed summer 2002, consists of the 18,000 square-foot two-level full service spa. The spa will further compliment the amenities of the resort and tie directly into the hotel's grotto pool and fitness center.

2

4 View of resort hotel from the 18th tee

5 Grotto pool below the main lobby. Pool overlooks lake at the 18th green

6 Grand stair at the conference center. Stair leads to lower level meeting rooms and terrace at the 18th green

Images: The Bissell Companies

5

4

7 Two-story main lobby with monumental arched
   window overlooking the golf course
8 Wood-paneled library with limestone fireplace,
   off the main lobby
9 Golf course façade of resort hotel with two-story
   veranda off the lobby
Images:The Bissell Companies

1 Crossroads 20 theatre exterior in Cary,
  North Carolina
2 Palmetto Grande theatre lobby in Mt. Pleasant,
  South Carolina
3 Palmetto Grande theatre exterior in Mt. Pleasant,
  South Carolina
Images: Jim Sink Photography

1

Design/Completion 1999/2001
Southeastern United States
Consolidated Theatres
Range: from 42,000 square feet to 74,000 square feet
Various structures and building materials

Consolidated Theatres

Beginning in 1997, LS3P ASSOCIATES LTD. was commissioned by Consolidated Theatres to design their new theatres in an extensive expansion throughout the Southeast. When LS3P ASSOCIATES LTD. began this foray into entertainment architecture, the president of Consolidated Theatres presented the firm a unique challenge. His was a strong regional chain facing stiff competition in his home market from the much larger national chains. To be successful, he felt his theatres had to provide an experience superior to his competition. With everyone showing the same movies, he felt that the buildings themselves were the key to success. Our challenge was to create the aura of the great movie palaces of the past, with no two being alike. In its projects, LS3P ASSOCIATES LTD. designed to state-of-the-art standards, including stadium seating, surround sound systems and projection systems, and a variety of concession merchandise outlets.

The buildings were highly thematic with the exterior architecture typically derived from the architecture of the surrounding development. From that would evolve the highly fanciful, romantic interiors focusing on main lobby areas where patrons congregate, wait for movie start times, view previews, eat at the concessions and people watch.

2

3

4

4   Crossroads 20 theatre lobby in Cary, North Carolina
5   Manchester Cinemas concessions in Rock Hill,
      South Carolina
6   Commonwealth 20 theatre lobby in Richmond,
      Virginia
7   Commonwealth 20 theatre exterior in Richmond,
      Virginia
Images: Jim Sink Photography

6

5

7

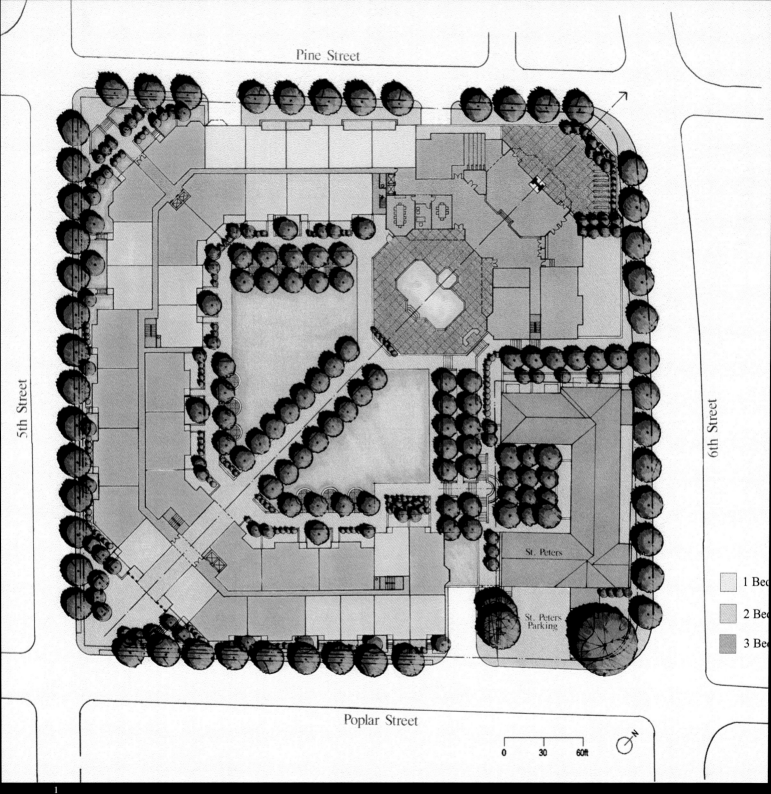

Pine Street

5th Street

6th Street

St. Peters

St. Peters
Parking

Poplar Street

1 Bed

2 Bed

3 Bed

0   30   60ft

N

Design/Completion 1999/2003
Charlotte, North Carolina
Spectrum Properties
540,000 square feet
Post tension, cast-in-place concrete, cast stone, brick veneer, stucco, slate and standing seam copper roofing

Fifth & Poplar Residential Complex

The project consists of an eight-story mid-rise residential tower located on the city block northwest of the intersection of Fifth Street and Poplar Street in uptown Charlotte. Two sub-levels of parking provide approximately 375 parking spaces on site below the residential building of approximately 350,000 square feet. At the lowest street level, retail shops of approximately 22,000 square feet, including an 18,000 square-foot grocery store, provide essential services for the complex and surrounding community. Two sides of the building base allow for street level residential units (brownstones) with sidewalk access. The residential tower wraps around the perimeter of the block creating a private interior garden plaza with fountains, walking paths, benches, a swimming pool and pool terrace, plus lawn areas at the center of the block above the parking structure. Residential units consist of 16 studio units, 137 one-bedroom units, 105 two-bedroom units, six three-bedroom units plus 40 penthouse suites.

1   Site plan
2   Corner of Fifth and Poplar
Images: LS3P ASSOCIATES LTD. (1); Risden McElroy (2)

2

3   Sixth Street elevation
4   Poplar Street elevation
5   Fifth Street elevation
6   Pine Street elevation
Images: LS3P ASSOCIATES LTD.

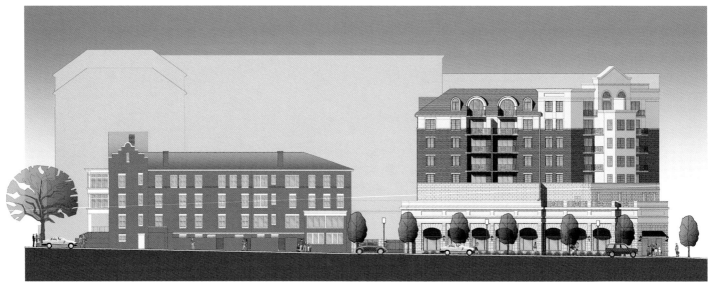

3

4

5

6

0   100ft

7

7   Corner of Pine and Sixth
8   Courtyard
Images: Risden McElroy

8

1

1 View of spiral stair
2 Exterior view from east
3 Entrance view
Images: Rick Alexander & Associates, Inc.

Design/Completion 1988/1989
Kiawah Island, South Carolina
Kiawah Resort Associates
8,975 square feet
Wood frame, cypress siding, metal roof

Kiawah Sales and Information Center

The Plantation House form of the Lowcountry of South Carolina provided the inspiration for this sales and information center for a barrier island resort. The double-sloped roof form which signifies and defines the quintessential modest plantation house of the South with its attached porch was used to define and separate the functions of offices from display areas. A gridded curtain-wall system continued the suggestion of a porch and affords the sales offices emphasized views of the island environs. The telescope massing of the facility is accented by the stepped painted standing seam 'tin' roof with stepped dormers.

The center mass culminates in a three-sided sales room of glass, which projects into a pond to afford 180-degree vistas to the prospective buyer.

Careful attention to siting and landscape treatment reinforce the quality of life on the island and create references back to plantation precedents. Set amid live oaks, crepe myrtles, palmettos, azaleas, and bountiful flowering annuals, the formal low and long approach prepares the guest for the hospitality and beauty of the island. The association of the building to the past continues with the interiors, which feature reclaimed heart-pine floors, twelve-foot ceilings, carefully detailed moulding and trim, oriental rugs, and custom-designed furniture. A pair of gracefully sweeping freestanding stairs flank the main entrance and reinforce the historical associations, while providing a dramatic ascension to the second floor.

2

3

Design/Completion 1998/2000
Charleston, South Carolina
BlueGreen Corporation
104,325 square feet
Existing wood and masonry, wood, masonry, stucco

Lodge Alley Inn Renovation

As a unique reminder of Charleston's past, the Lodge Alley Inn occupies several historic warehouses in one the city's oldest districts. Previously renovated to accommodate a hotel in 1982, the current renovation sought to restore the charm of the past while addressing the amenity expectations of the sophisticated timeshare owner.

Renovating the inn into a marketable timeshare required major restoration of the existing infrastructure including all mechanical, electrical and structural systems. Working with the Preservation Society and the local Board of Architectural Review, these necessary alterations were carefully detailed to minimize any visual distraction from the charm of the inn.

The new renovation of the inn has attracted many newcomers to historical downtown Charleston. The thoughtful design renovation of the property has paid high dividends for the timeshare company while maintaining its historical significance to downtown Charleston.

1   Exterior view of Griffith Suites and courtyard
2   Reception/entry lobby
Images: Rick Alexander & Associates, Inc.

2

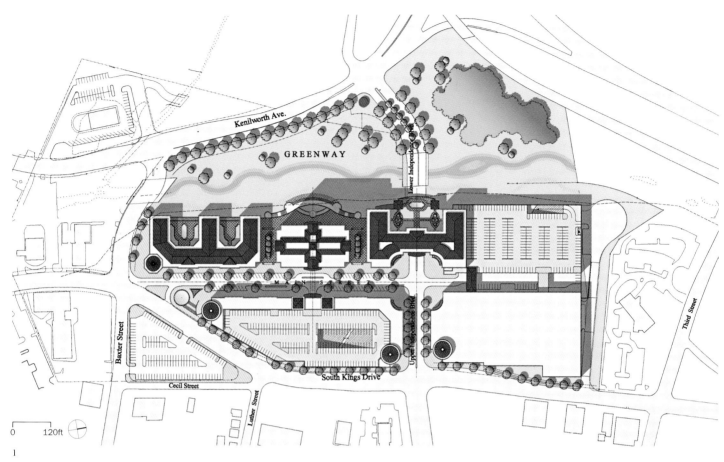

1

2

Design/Completion 1999/ongoing
Charlotte, North Carolina
Pappas Properties, LLC
25-acre site

Midtown Square Master Plan

In 1999, LS3P ASSOCIATES LTD. was commissioned by Pappas Properties, LLC to master plan an urban mixed-use development at Midtown, a 25-acre site adjacent to Uptown Charlotte. The site was the home of Charlottetown Mall, the city's first enclosed mall dating to the early 1960s. The new project's key components consist of retail, including national anchors and local shops, offices and multi-family residential (both rental and condominium), and parking structures.

The plan called for the creation of an internal Main Street as the development's central organizing element. One of the key design elements of the plan is uncovering Little Sugar Creek, which was decked over with the original mall. This stream corridor will become a public park and centerpiece of a continuous greenway, running from Uptown Charlotte to the South Carolina state line. An under-utilized state thoroughfare, Independence

Boulevard, which bisects the site, will become a private street providing major vehicular access to the project.

To the north of Independence Boulevard will be the major retail anchors, 'stacked' in a two-story building. Across the Main Street from these 'stacked boxes' will be the parking structure, accommodating their required parking.

The adjacent condominium building bridges the boulevard, creating a monumental entry portal to the site.

South of Independence will be a 300,000 square-foot office tower and rental multi-family residential building, both with street level retail. The siting of both buildings takes advantage of the Charlotte Center City skyline beyond the greenway park. Parking for these two components is planned on the opposite side of Main Street in a central parking structure. The parking structure along Main Street will be lined with residential units and continuous street-level retail. The opposite face of the parking structure will provide service-type retail and live-work units on Kings Drive, the major thoroughfare along the project's eastern edge.

1 Master plan showing the greenway to the west and Main Street in project's center
2 Approach view along Independence Boulevard with condominium building terminating entry vista
3 Partial elevation of central parking structure along Kings Drive. Elevation shows retail entry at corner with façade of deck above
Images: LS3P ASSOCIATES LTD. (1,3);
Risden McElroy (2)

3

1   Aerial rendering of Morrocroft Centre showing reflecting pool and garden with Morrison Regional Library in foreground
2   Morrocroft One: entry façade from the garden
3   Morrocroft Two from Colony Road
4   Portico at Morrocroft One

Images: Risden McElroy (1); Gordon H. Schenck, Jr. Photography (2,4); Rick Alexander & Associates, Inc. (3)

Design/Completion 1990/2000
Charlotte, North Carolina
The Bissell Companies, The Harris Group, Lincoln Harris
Three 100,000 square-foot office buildings; two parking decks with 970 spaces
Office Buildings: steel frame, brick, cast stone, glass and acrylic stucco ornamentation
Parking Decks: precast concrete

Morrocroft Centre

Morrocroft, the first suburban mixed-use development in Charlotte, is located in the city's SouthPark area. The mixed-use components include high-end single family residential and the 26-acre commercial district, which LS3P ASSOCIATES LTD. master-planned and designed. This commercial center consists of specialty retail, an office complex, and the city's first regional library. Each of the three components occupies its own individual parcel, with different ownership groups in place as each phase developed. The master plan layers the various uses along a central north-south axis with Morrocroft Village, the retail component along the northern edge, adjacent to SouthPark Mall and Sharon Road, one of the area's major thoroughfares.

The office component, Morrocroft Centre, occupies the larger central zone of the site. Morrocroft Centre consists of three 100,000 square-foot office buildings supported by two parking structures of 970 cars. The office buildings are clustered around an axial reflecting pool and formal par-terre garden that acts as the public space for the complex.

South of Morrocroft Centre and the terminus to the north-south axis, forming the southern edge for the reflecting pool garden, is the Morrison Regional Library. This civic building transitions the Morrocroft's commercial center to the surrounding single-family neighborhoods. This north-south axis visually unites the project's three components and establishes the primary connection between the three uses.

A common architectural aesthetic, a Jeffersonian-inspired classical language, was prescribed by the project developers. This language was used throughout to provide the entire development with a distinctive visual identity. Classically-derived elements were located along the central axis to visually denote each component. These include the monumental arch that serves as a ceremonial portal from Sharon Road into the Morrocroft Village retail complex, the central portico of the major office building overlooking the bronze sculpture in the reflecting pool, and the library, designed as a Palladian 'Five Part' plan villa with its central pavilion surmounted with a low dome.

3

4

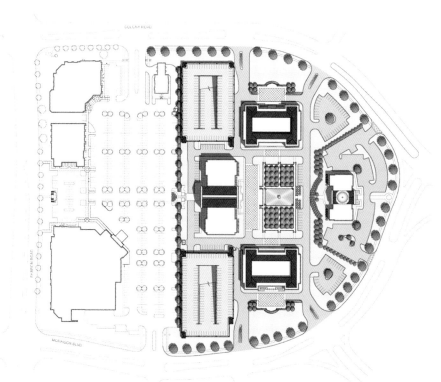

5 Site plan

6 View of Morrocroft Centre and reflecting pool from library with Morrocroft One on axis

7 Morrocroft One: entry with motor-court in foreground

Following pages:

Morrocroft One and Two facing the reflecting pool and par-terre garden

Images: LS3P ASSOCIATES LTD. (5);
Rick Alexander & Associates, Inc. (6, following pages);
Gordon H. Schenck, Jr. Photography (7)

5

0   100ft

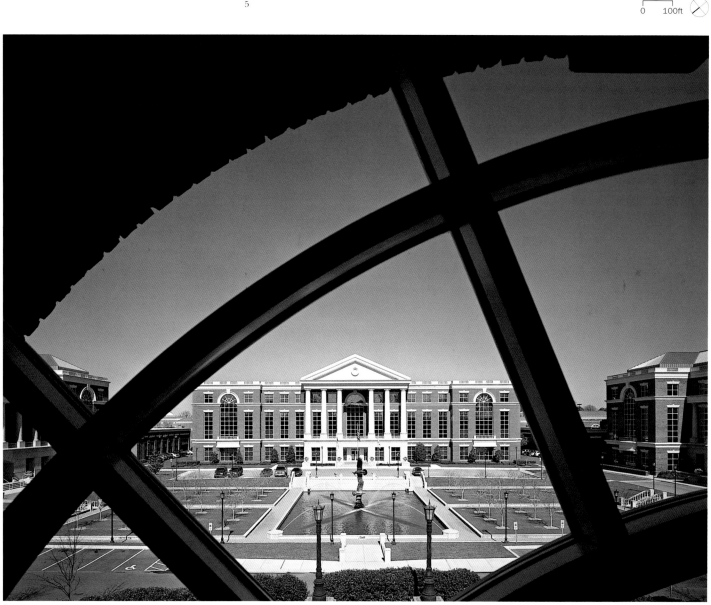

6

146

1

Design/Completion 1993/2000
Charlotte, North Carolina
The Harris Group
100,000 square feet of retail/restaurant space; a 30,000 square-foot 10-plex movie theater; a 124-suite
hotel; 430 multi family residential units; and 550 parking spaces in three associated parking structures
Retail/restaurant buildings: steel frame, limestone water table and water table cap
Theater: insulated precast panels with concrete tees at the roof, acrylic stucco walls and ornamental trim
Hotel: CMU wall construction with poured slab floors, aluminum-clad wood windows and standing seam
metal roof
Residential units: wood frame over cast concrete street retail, wood siding, brick veneer and acrylic stucco
Parking structure: precast concrete

Phillips Place Lifestyle Center

Phillips Place occupies a 35-acre site that was the largest undeveloped tract in the SouthPark area of Charlotte. The goal of the development was to refine the transition from the enclosed SouthPark mall area and its surrounding office buildings to the multi-family and single-family residential neighborhoods located to the east and south of the Fairview corridor.

The major components of Phillips Place are 100,000 square feet of retail/restaurant space; a 30,000 square-foot 10-plex movie theater; a 124-suite hotel; and 430 multi-family residential units. The vision for Phillips Place was to truly integrate these components into a unique, pedestrian-friendly environment organized around an interior 'main street', Phillips Place Court. Bordered by tree-lined sidewalks, the street was designed for two-way automobile traffic with angled parking on each side. The north side of this street contains retail/restaurant spaces designed to accommodate second-level mezzanine space. The south side consists of three-story buildings comprised of ground-level retail with multi-family housing in a mixture of two-story townhouses and flats. The mass of these buildings provide the necessary enclosure to the street and its

pedestrian promenades to make Phillips Place Court a pleasing, public, outdoor living room for the entire development. Phillips Place Court terminates at small courts with specially designed cast stone fountains. The theater anchors the eastern terminus and the six-story hotel anchors the west.

A series of controlled spaces creates a secondary north/south axis that crosses the main axis of Phillips Place Court at its midpoint. An open-air galleria frames the vista of Phillips Place Court to Fairview Road. Immediately to the south is a central square which allows for outdoor entertainment and dining, open to balcony views from the upper story apartments. South of the square is a private garden court framed by residential buildings.

Parking for the project is distributed around the perimeter of Phillips Place Court and its adjacent buildings. The natural slope of the site allows for two-level tray-type decks to the south. This placement allows for a concentration of parking at the theater and provides secured residential parking on the lower-level of the project's center with retail parking above.

The buildings are designed in a simple classical palette establishing a visual cohesion to the project. Different coloration of the synthetic stucco of the wall surfaces allows variety within the general order of the architectural pallet. Complimentary-colored canvas awnings also contribute to the visual variety.

2

1   Terminus fountain court at hotel
2   Shop front at public courtyard off Phillips
    Place Court
Images: Rick Alexander & Associates, Inc.

3

4

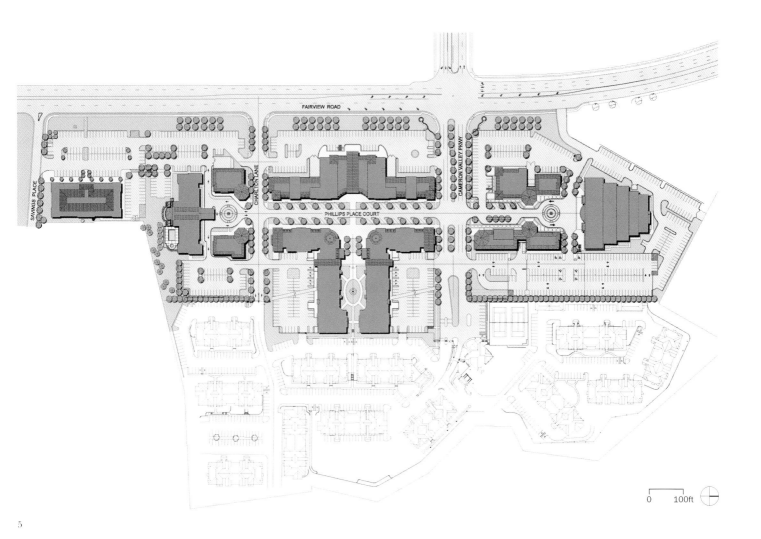

FAIRVIEW ROAD

PHILLIPS PLACE COURT

0   100ft

5

7 Private residential courtyard looking back toward entry gallery
8 Typical storefronts along Phillips Place Court with residential above
9 Two-story retail on north side of Phillips Place Court

Following pages:
    Theatre at terminus fountain court

Images: Rick Alexander & Associates, Inc.

8

7

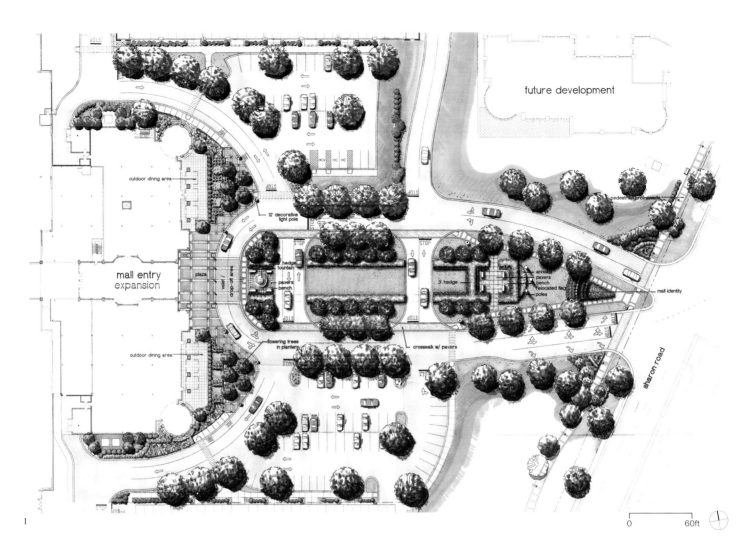

future development

outdoor dining area

mall entry
expansion

plaza

12' decorative
light pole

hedge
fountain

pavers
bench

outdoor dining area

flowering trees
in planters

annual
pavers
bench
relocated flag
poles

3' hedge

mall identity

crosswalk w/ pavers

pedestrian promenade

sharon road

0   60ft

1

LTD

2

Design/Completion phased completions November 2002 through March 2004
Charlotte, North Carolina
Simon Property Group
1.7 million square feet at final phase
Precast concrete and steel, stone water tables, stucco detailing, glass canopies, and exposed metalwork
Additional Credit: LandDesign (Master Planning)

SouthPark Regional Mall

Located in the heart of the third largest office center in the Carolinas, SouthPark offers high-end shopping to the fast growing region it surrounds. A conscious move was made to transform the 70s-era suburban mall into a community-friendly social center featuring pedestrian-friendly connections between components and the neighborhoods. The corners of the site, formerly open parking lots, have been redefined with architectural structures joined by linear parks. The new crown jewel in the center is the main entrance structure with an open glass gallery and dome. One corner will host up to 18,000 people for symphony summer pops concerts at a dedicated park and unique band shell structure. Another incorporates living units over retail, fronting a street and village green complete with sidewalk cafes. The transformation is representative of the zeal to accommodate a pedestrian-oriented lifestyle with all the amenities associated with being able to walk from here to there. At the same time the main entrance, a 75-foot high crystal dome, presides over the entire site trumpeting the theatrics and excitement of shopping. The classical infrastructure responds to the community's demands for town identity while the glass and metalwork overlays talk high fashion.

1   Main entrance boulevard landscape plan
2   Outdoor dining at Holiday Park
3   Main entry gallery
Images: LandDesign (1); Risden McElroy (2,3)

3

4

5

4   Holiday Park, a residential and retail complex
5   Main entrance boulevard
6   Illustrative site plan
7   Concert pavilion at Symphony Park
8   Corner fountain at Holiday Park

Images: Risden McElroy (4,5,7,8);
LS3P ASSOCIATES LTD. (6)

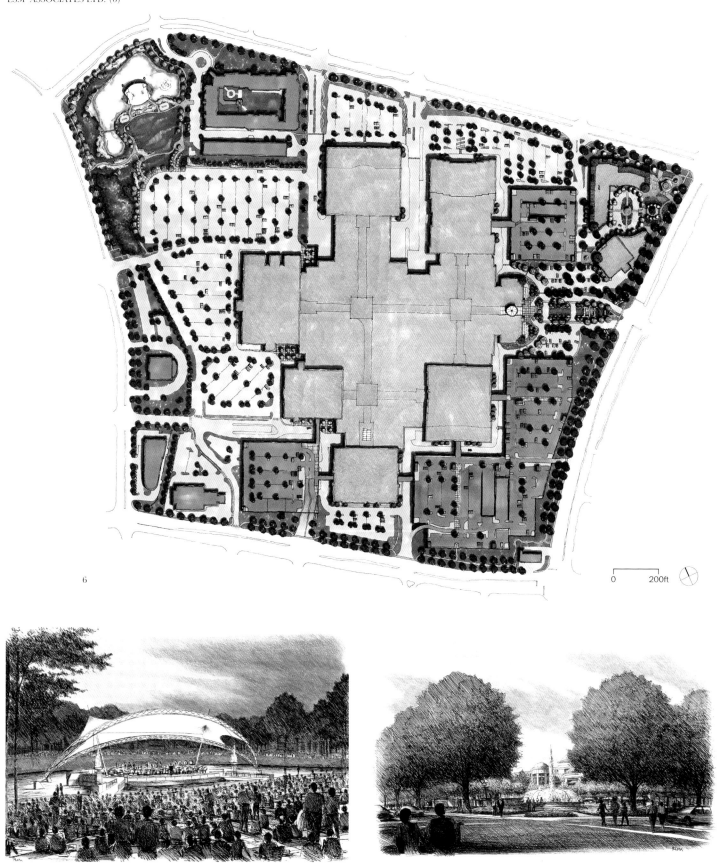

6

0   200ft

7   8

Design/Completion 1988/1989
Isle of Palms, South Carolina
Wild Dunes Development
Wood framing, wood siding and decking, metal roofing

Wild Dunes Resort Grand Pavilion

This project is included as part of the master planning of a small beach community patterned after turn-of-the-century ocean-front towns. The tightly-knit site plan includes various cottage designs which front on either the ocean, community decks, pools, a boardwalk, or the croquet lawns. An ocean-front beach deck with two pools flanking an open-air pavilion provides a community gathering space with a spectacular view of the ocean.

A raised boardwalk, off of which future cottages will open, links the beach deck and pavilion to another pool complex which has changing rooms, showers, and shade structures. Careful selection of materials, landscaping, and details helps to establish a sense of community while allowing for variety in the individual cottage designs.

1 View of pavilion from beach
2 View from beach
3 Boardwalk view
Images: Gordon H. Schenck, Jr. Photography

2

3

Opposite:
    Arbor at rest rooms and showers
5   Master plan
Images: Gordon H. Schenck, Jr. Photography
(opposite); LS3P ASSOCIATES LTD. (5)

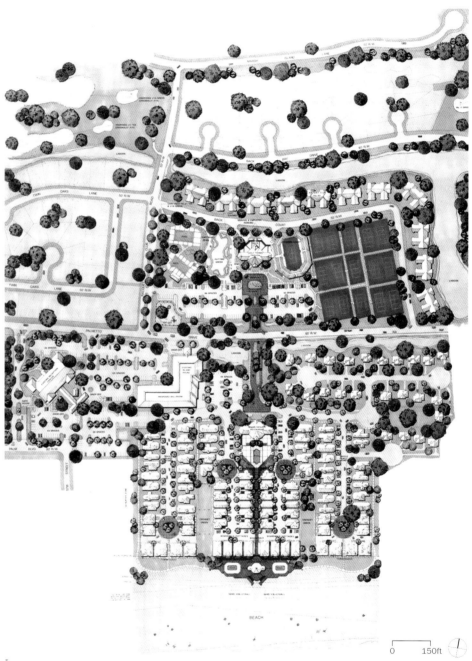

5

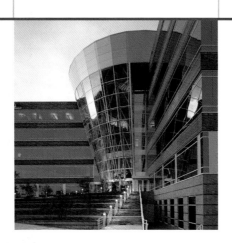

OFFICE BUILDINGS

Atrium at Blue Ridge

Charleston Gateway Center

Crestar Riverview Center

The Ellipse at Harris Corners

Palmetto Electric Cooperative Inc.

Parkdale Mills Corporate Headquarters

Piggly Wiggly Corporate Headquarters

Regional Banking Center

Saks Majestic Square Complex

Springs Mills Executive Office Building

Design/Completion 1993/1997
Raleigh, North Carolina
Blue Ridge Realty
150,000 square feet
Composite steel and concrete framing, brick veneer, aluminum curtain wall and high-performance glazing

Atrium at Blue Ridge

Centrally located in an office park campus at the intersection of Blue Ridge Road and Lake Boone Trail, this five-story, class 'A' office building occupies an uneven site. The parking structure, located to the south and lower side of the site so as not to impose upon tenant views, is connected with a pedestrian bridge to the office building at the second level of the office.

The basic plan is L-shaped with a conical-shaped atrium located at the confluence of the two wings. The atrium incorporates glass-enclosed elevators and an elliptical skylight. The elevator movement adds visual excitement to the public spaces. The exposed steel framing of the bridge and atrium, with the tinted glass, gives a crisp and dramatic high-tech image that compliments the flush reflective glass and smooth brick of the main body of the building.

Opposite:
    Atrium entrance
2   Main entrance façade
Images: Marc Lamkin

2

3 Bridge connector between parking structure
  and office building
4 Atrium skylight
Images: Marc Lamkin

3

Design/Completion 1993/1997
Charleston, South Carolina
Rivers Enterprises
80,000 square feet
Steel frame, precast concrete, glass

Charleston Gateway Center

Opposite:
    Detail of entry pavilion
2   Rooftop garden pavilion
Images: Rick Alexander & Associates, Inc.

The nearness of this office building to the harbor, with its marine industrial activity and resultant port-oriented vocabulary, dictated that this design show more use allegiance to that component of the city than to its more historic areas further away from the water. This condition was the single most important dictate in the design for this new building. The late 19th and early 20th-century marine industrial buildings close to the development evidenced large areas of glass with small amounts of crudely finished exterior wall between. The design alludes to these buildings while at the same time creating highly-finished Class 'A' office space. The overriding proportion of all the city's old buildings is vertical, and as such, is decidedly different from a horizontal office building. The solution was to use dark reveals at the structural columns to impose a rhythm of strong vertical proportions onto the horizontal building. In this way, especially from the pedestrian point of view, the building appears as a series of smaller vertical buildings more in keeping with the historic structures commonly found elsewhere in the city.

2

3   South elevation showing sun control devices
4   Entry pavilion at south elevation
Images: Rick Alexander & Associates, Inc.

3

4

Opposite:
  Two-story entry lobby
6 Entry pavilion
Images: Rick Alexander & Associates, Inc.

1

1   Evening shot of entrance cylinder across plaza
2   View across James River from the north
3   Detail at visitors' entrance into cylinder from the
     level below the plaza

Images: Joann Sieburg-Baker (1,3);
The Photo Link/Larry Olsen (2)

Design/Completion 1995/1998
Richmond, Virginia
Crestar Bank
411,120 square-foot office and 516,713 square-foot parking garage for a total of 927,833 square feet
Sand blasted precast concrete, white painted aluminum panel, and Low-E coating on clear glass

Crestar Riverview Center

This six-story Bank Operations Center, located across the James River from the central business district of Richmond, Virginia, includes a 1,300-car underground parking structure, a 411,120 square-foot office building, and a garden plaza on top of a portion of the underground parking. The office building, housing the consumer finance operations for a major bank, occupies a two-block, nearly-square site overlooking the falls of the James River. It reflects the bank's desire to combine several existing operations into a single structure that provides limited public access to a secure site and building.

Banking functions dictated a design providing a secure operations facility with a large, flexible plan. The program called for a building with efficient and direct access from the existing Mortgage Building on the adjacent block to employee amenities housed in the new facility and secure and direct access into the building from the parking structure.

These goals, along with the site topography, generated two extensive ground floor levels. The underground level accommodates general delivery services, a large mail center, parking entrances for the below-grade parking, and employee access from the Mortgage Building into the cylinder. The main ground level provides visitor parking at the garden plaza. Public access into the building is through a main, secure entrance at the cylinder, opening into a double-height lobby which includes elevators from parking, a guard station, and main building elevators. The main ground floor circulation is a two-story gallery connecting the cylinder to facilities such as the 500-person cafeteria, general training, and exercise areas. Elevator cores located at the cylinder and near the entrance to the cafeteria anticipate and encourage the flow of employees to and from these amenities through both the gallery and the courtyard.

On the James River elevation the base of the building acts as a podium that provides a continuous balcony accessible from public spaces, such as the cafeteria, on the main entry level. The scale of the building on the river façade is broken into four equal segments each with a wave-like curvature to reflect the motion of the water below. At night the lighted entrance cylinder acts as a beacon that is visible from the city center of Richmond across the river.

2

3

4 Site plan
5 Vertical perspective of entrance cylinder
Following pages:
    Entrance cylinder and east façade
Images: LS3P ASSOCIATES LTD. (4);
The Photo Link/Larry Olsen (5); Joann Sieburg-Baker
(following pages)

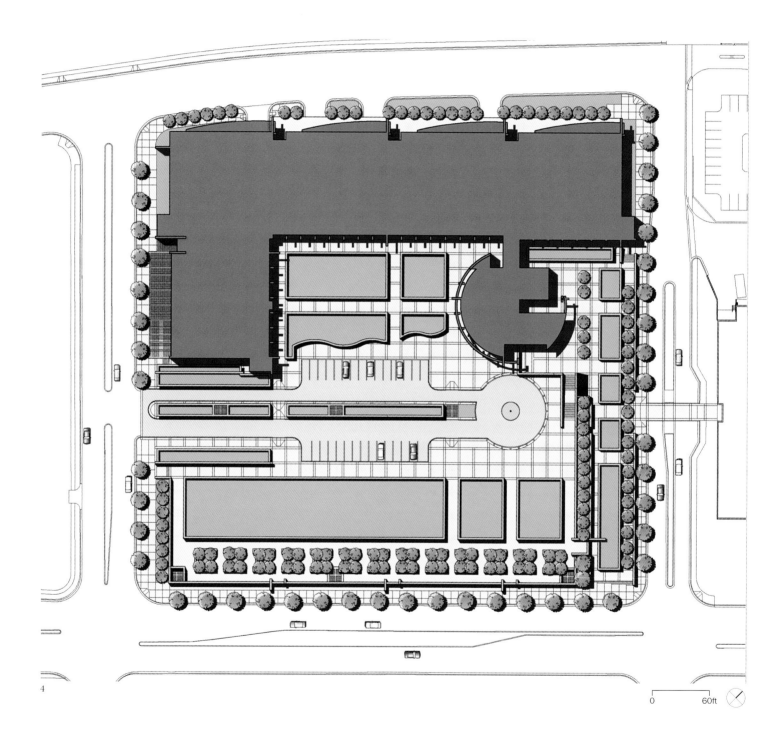

4

0   60ft

7 Corner detail of James River façade
8 Façade detail of secondary entrance
Opposite:
    Visitors' lobby and security desk
Images: The Photo Link/Larry Olsen (7,8);
Joann Sieburg-Baker (opposite)

8

7

10 First floor connector between visitors' lobby and
    employee cafeteria
11 Section, east/west through the parking levels,
    entry plaza and office building
12 Custom-designed rug in two-story pre-function
    area outside training area
Images: Joann Sieburg-Baker (10,12);
LS3P ASSOCIATES LTD. (11)

1   Entry façade from entry drive
2   Entry portal from motor court
3   Oblique view of entry façade
Images: Tim Buchman

1

2

Design/Completion 1998/Ongoing
Charlotte, North Carolina
Beacon Partners
125,000 square feet
Steel structure, architectural precast concrete with granite accents, reflective glass

The Ellipse at Harris Corners

In 1998, Beacon Partners commissioned LS3P ASSOCIATES LTD. to plan the transformation of their Harris Corners Business Park along the booming interstate highway I-77 north corridor in Charlotte, from a development of one-story flex space buildings into a class 'A' office environment with associated retail/restaurants and lodging components.

The centerpiece of this new master plan is the Ellipse, a two-building, 250,000 square-foot office complex designed around a public garden. Working within the existing road infrastructure, the Ellipse is planned to create a visual landscape focus for the corporate park that had previously been flat, featureless agricultural fields. Surface parking for the five-story office buildings is laid out in an elliptical pattern with the perimeter enclosed by an evergreen hedge broken at 20-foot intervals by columnar

Skyrocket Junipers. The buildings are aligned along a roughly diagonal axis that allows the entry façade and motor court of one building to gesture to the intersection of the two major public arteries that serve the site. The entry façade and motor court of the second building gesture towards northbound traffic along I-77. At the center of the axis is the actual ellipse, the public garden. The buildings' lobbies are along the short axis of the garden with public pedestrian ways entering the garden from the long axis. At the crossing of these two axis is a fountain/water feature designed for this space as its visual focus. Around the fountain is an events lawn, capable of supporting park-wide social events. Around the events lawn is an elliptical garden path shaded by oak trees. This path provides for more passive use of the garden, with benches having data ports for computer access.

The buildings are designed with a more transitional architectural language, combining simplified traditional architectural forms with more contemporary elements, providing the 'buttoned-down' corporate aesthetic the developers were seeking. The primary building-surface materials are architectural precast and glass. The precast is stratified, with a retarded finish at the base, surrounded by heavy and medium sand-blasted areas above. A vertical tower element is created at the motor court and garden entries, to tie it to each axis. At the base, a large two-story granite portal signifies entry to the lobby. The tower is surmounted by a distinctive lighted pyramidal beacon.

3

4 Central vertical element from motor court at night
5 Perspective rendering showing complex at build-out
  with ellipse garden and motor court at entry
Opposite:
  Entry lobby with slightly domed ceiling
Images: Tim Buchman (4, opposite); Risden McElroy (5)

4

5

Design/Completion 1998/2002
Bluffton, South Carolina
Palmetto Electric Cooperative Inc.
39,000 square feet
Steel structure, slab on grade, brick and stucco, metal roof

Palmetto Electric Cooperative Inc.

This 39,000 square-foot office for Palmetto Electric Cooperative Inc. is located on a 14-acre site in Bluffton, South Carolina, a fast developing area outside of Hilton Head Island where the cooperative was formerly located. This structure, in the New River East Development, serves as both a regional office to serve the rural/suburban population of Beaufort and Jasper Counties, and a corporate headquarters containing executive, engineering, marketing, operations and information staff. This structure is designed with the importance factors associated with emergency support projects as it is an essential facility that will operate through most tropical weather. The facility has generators and UPS systems that allow the concrete-walled and roofed control center within to maintain knowledge of the thousands of miles of utility lines in Palmetto Electric's service area.

While the client is technologically sophisticated, the Cooperative needed to maintain a traditional appearance for its members, contractors and vendors visiting this facility. Brick and stucco are combined with metal-framed translucent panels to give the simultaneous feeling of lightness and stability. A two-story spine with clerestory allows daylight into the main corridor and projects through the two-story lobby into the landscape as a porch joining the inside and outside.

1   Pedestrian walkway covered by translucent panels
2   View of office building across detention pond
3   Stucco element protecting lobby from southern exposure
Images: Rick Alexander & Associates, Inc.

3

4

5

6

4   Stucco spine intersecting office structure and
    porch element
5   Interior view of conference/meeting room adjacent
    to lobby
6   One-story porch at lobby
Images: Rick Alexander & Associates, Inc.

Design/Completion 1998/2001
Gastonia, North Carolina
Parkdale Mills
45,000 square feet
Steel frame, brick, aluminum curtain wall, Low-E and clear glass

Parkdale Mills Corporate Headquarters

The brief was to design a 45,000 square-foot World Corporate Headquarters for a textile manufacturer, which would create efficient relationships between departments and create a forum for ideas. The new headquarters brings together departments previously spread throughout the county. The concept supports these goals by creating an office environment, which is open and accessible, clear in its organization and welcoming to its users.

The site is a 25-acre wooded hourglass-shaped parcel adjacent to a major thoroughfare. In contrast to the existing structures along the thoroughfare, this building is set back from the street, creating a V-shaped view corridor. The geometry of the site plan accommodates a new public street that skirts the perimeter of the site. This organization provides two future building sites to the southwest and northeast.

The heart of the building is a great central room, an abstraction of a cone of yarn, which soars vertically through the roof.

2

The cone, which houses an exhibit on the history of cotton, connects the two main floors and defines the programmatic elements on each floor. This lofty light-filled volume, on axis with the main entrance to the north, and employee entrance to the south, serves both to identify the corporation to the outside world and to provide a focus for life within the building.

The concept arranges the program in a compact pavilion that addresses the existing landscape and the new superimposed order. The first floor is comprised of a lobby and exhibit area, technical support and general services, open office and five private parking spaces within the mechanical pavilion. The executive offices, with waiting area and conference rooms, look through the cone on the second floor to the open office area.

Externally the façade is a juxtaposition of glass and brick. Within the façade, an asymmetrical series of elements portray activities inside the building. The cone, the curtain wall and the brick wall with ribbon windows combine to build a horizontal composition. The façade combines components of a larger module outer skin, inner planning module and large smooth-face brick panels to create a layered reading at multiple scales. The clear glass skin in the open office areas allows north daylight to be shared by all.

1   Evening shot of the transparent two-story employee wing of the corporate headquarters building
2   Connector stair and bridge from parking through mechanical support building
3   Interior courtyard between support building (left) and corporate headquarters building (right)
Images: Tim Buchman

3

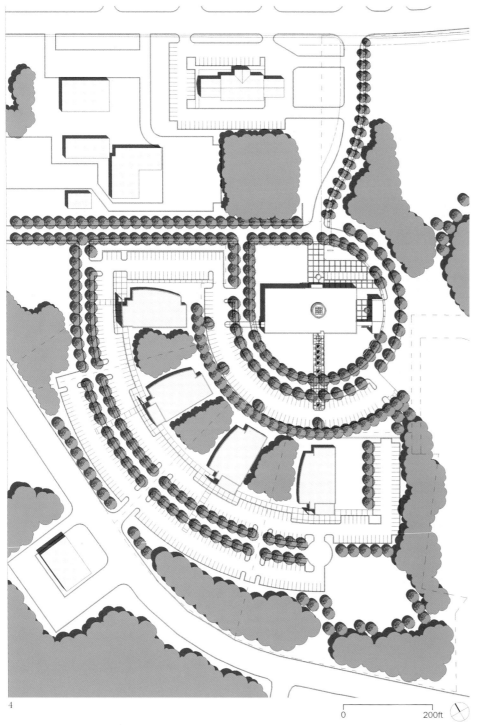

4   Site plan
5   Apex of entrance cone showing clerestory and
    skylight
6   Open plan executive support area
7   Detached support building and the main building
    housing executive areas in the east wing of the
    corporate headquarters building
Following pages:
    Entrance cone at reception desk
Images: LS3P ASSOCIATES LTD. (4); Carolina Photo
Group/Larry Harwell (5,6, following pages);
Tim Buchman (7)

4

0   200ft

5

6

7

9   Executive conference room
10   Reception lobby and historical display
Images: Carolina Photo Group/Larry Harwell

9

10

Design/Completion 1996/1999
Charleston, South Carolina
Piggly Wiggly Company
77,000 square feet
Steel, brick, precast concrete and stucco

Piggly Wiggly Corporate Headquarters

Albemarle Point Center is a four-story office building across the Ashley River from Charleston and its top floors enjoy views of the nearby harbor. The building was mandated by the city to be respectful of the scale and materials of nearby suburban neighborhoods of largely traditional design character. Addressing the scale issue was the principal challenge, and this was accomplished by faceting the building's mass into a symmetrically balanced series of setbacks eroding the bulk of the structure into smaller-scale pieces. The relationship of the building to the traditions of Charleston architecture was addressed by employing the classically-ordered vertical separation of base, middle, and attic story to break down the building's scale into more manageable components, which the most immediately affected residential neighborhoods and the city itself, found successful.

The owner and principal tenant of the building, Piggly Wiggly, is a Carolina-based food retailer. The company's public spaces, clad in a rich palette of materials, feature a spacious formal reception area with two large conference rooms and a gallery to provide an historical overview of the organization.

The reception/waiting area makes a memorable first impression. The 10-foot, 360-degree circular Sapele wood reception desk features a black granite transaction top with an inset panel of Moabi pomelle set in a reverse diamond pattern. The main conference room is fully equipped with state-of-the-art audiovisual and telecommunications equipment cleverly concealed within feature millwork pieces

to maintain a clean appearance. The circular gallery, designed to give a historical overview of the company, contains recessed display boxes expertly contoured to fit the radius of the room. Each box interior is covered in fabric. Focused lighting with back-recessed illumination emphasizes the objects on display.

To bring light into the corridors, borrowed lights were designed for each office surrounding the perimeter of the building. 'Blind-glass' was used within the frames to give visual privacy to the occupants from the corridor. Jamb assemblies were clamped and glued around drywall partitions to avoid face nailing. Makore wood stile-and-rail assemblies were designed with an infield of figured Sapele wood and acoustical or tackable fabric panels.

To maintain a clean appearance in the public areas, full-height hidden door panels opening into service areas (such as closets and pantries) were designed to avoid distraction from major features of the rooms. The large panels also conceal audiovisual and teleconferencing equipment with white board screens used during strategic planning events.

One of the greatest challenges faced by the designer was the client's request to incorporate the corporate logo, 'Mr. Pig', into the office suite. Carving and sandblasting the logo on both sides of a five-foot by 11-foot piece of tempered glass tastefully accomplished this. The frameless glass panel is secured at the top and bottom only. Lighting is recessed into the ceiling above the glass, and penetrates down the surface, illuminating the carved portions and creating a subtle dimensional tone-on-tone affect. The logo was also used discreetly in the signage where the image was engraved into a dropped box on a stainless steel header bar.

1   Main entry detail
2   Entry façade, west side
3   Frameless, internally-lit, sandblasted glass panel
    with company's logo
Images: Rick Alexander & Associates, Inc.

4

5

4   View into main corridor and reception area
5   Reception/waiting area
Opposite:
    Main conference room
Images: Rick Alexander & Associates, Inc.

1

1   View of northeast corner at bank entry
2   Main banking floor
Images: Rick Alexander & Associates, Inc.

Design/Completion 1989/1991
Charleston, South Carolina
First Union National Bank
70,000 square feet
Steel with moment connections for seismic design, granite base and stucco on the upper floors

Regional Banking Center

The site for this project occurs at one of the most significant and well-known intersections within the historic district of Charleston, South Carolina. The building design exhibits a blending of the bank's desire to have a contemporary image, while accommodating the historicist posture of the city's Architectural Review Board.

The building design evolved from the three principal parts of the program: the renovation of the 1835 Madren Building, the bank building at the corner, and the commercial and retail space proceeding west on Market Street. These three parts are both unified as a whole and emphasized by continuous notches of glass, which join the parts.

To follow historical patterns of corner buildings in Charleston, the building strongly addresses the corner with the bank's principal entrance, while opening it up for visibility and ease of entry.

Materials of the building underscore and reinforce not only the nature of Charleston but the nature of banking institutions.

The tri-partite division of elevations is emphasized through a granite base and the planes of stucco on the upper floors, while granite and marble floors combine with cherry and mahogany woodwork and liberal use of wrought iron on the interior.

2

Design/Completion 1993/1996
Charleston, South Carolina
The Beach Company
285,000 square feet
Post-tensioned concrete, brick, limestone-colored precast concrete

Saks Majestic Square Complex

Majestic Square, which takes its name from the old Majestic Theatre, is a 285,000 square-foot building composed of retail, office, and parking deck. The scale of this building presented the design team with a considerable challenge to make it an integral component of the small-scale shopping street, and a welcome neighbor to the nearby residential streets to the west, and to the Riviera Theatre to the north.

It was desirable that there would be no expression of the 600-car garage visible from the front half of the building. This is the reason that the three office levels above Saks Fifth Avenue are 'wrapped' around and above the three principal parking levels. The building's exterior vertical expression relates to the general height of adjacent King Street buildings by emphasizing the first 30 feet with a change of materials at that point.

The corner expression speaks to the era of grand mercantile structures from the late 19th century, as seen in great cities all over America, and fills that gap in the commercial district's streetscape, while the smaller scale of the first two floors continues the richness of detail seen for most of this storied retail street's length.

2

Opposite:
 Northeast corner at entry to Saks
2 King Street context
Images: Rick Alexander & Associates, Inc.

5

3   Detail
4   Detail of Market Street (north) façade
5   South access alley for deck
Images: Rick Alexander & Associates, Inc.

4

6 Detail of Market Street garage entry and shops
fronting deck
7 Mid-block office tenant entry lobby
Images: Rick Alexander & Associates, Inc.

6

1

1 Atrium detail from garden façade
2 Interior of atrium connecting stair from new entry
  to second floor
3 New garden façade with employee cafeteria on
  lower level
4 Interior of atrium from third floor
Images: Carolina Photo Group/Larry Harwell

Design/Completion Dates 1993/1999
Fort Mill, South Carolina
Springs Industries, Inc.
86,000 square feet
Steel construction, brick, clear anodized aluminum framing with Low-E insulated glazing

Springs Mills Executive Office Building

The design concept was developed in response to the owner's requirement for the creation of a new architectural expression that symbolized the importance of communication between the various departments in the renovation of this 1950s corporate headquarters for a Fortune 500 company. This architectural image was to complement the graceful rounded corners of the original building.

Transforming the original, closed, almost windowless facility into a transparent and vertically-connected office environment was achieved by the insertion of a three-story atrium entry space that created a new 'Interior Corporate Commons' for all employees. The atrium space was defined by the demolition of a 30 foot-wide by 80 foot-long bay of the existing building on all three floors. The replacement of the structure with an interconnecting, sky-lit, slate-clad stair, winding through the new floors, resulted in the creation of a central focal point and orientation element connecting the two office floors with the garden level cafeteria and sculpture garden.

The interior material finish selections were based on materials found elsewhere in the existing facility and are in keeping with the spirit of the building's 1950 design. The original corporate design utilized stainless steel ornamental railings that recalled railings found on the airships of the 1940s. Many newly-created architectural elements were also based on aeronautical designs of the era.

The completed design solution addresses all of the client's objectives in a manner that integrates the circulation patterns and the view from and into the atrium, with a symbolic emphasis on a new garden. This was created to display a bronze sculpture depicting a key value of the corporate philosophy, 'creativity', represented by a man and woman engaged in an interactive dialogue concerning design issues for a future company product.

TECHNOLOGY

Cannon Street Medical Office Building

Joe Gibbs Racing Facility

Medical University of South Carolina Storm Eye Institute

Roper Hospital Bratney Atrium

Trident Palmetto Hematology Oncology Clinic

Westvaco Charleston Technical Center

Westvaco Forest Research Complex

1

2

1 Exterior entry façade with terrace
2 Building entry and waiting vestibule
3 Entry colonnade/screen wall
4 Atrium and elevator lobby
Images: Rick Alexander & Associates, Inc.

Design/Completion 1999/2002
Charleston, South Carolina
The Beach Company
78,000 square feet
Post-tensioned concrete, stucco, brick and aluminum metal panels

Cannon Street Medical Office Building

This 78,000 square-foot medical office building is located within the city's historic district and serves an adjacent academic medical complex. Four floors house research physicians' offices and clinics as well as medical administration. The design of the building was meant to evoke a transitional vocabulary between the historic context of the site and the cutting edge technology of the researchers housed within.

In relating to the residential character of the area, the building became a good neighbor as well as a catalyst to promote urban renewal and surrounding rehabilitation. The two-story precast colonnade/screen wall on the north façade acts as the transitional element between the nearby homes and the four-story office. The building materials of stucco and brick reflect the 19th-century development of Charleston while the addition of more updated aluminum metal panels are used to emphasis the 21st-century medical research that occurs within.

3

4

Design/Completion 1997/1998
Huntersville, North Carolina
Joe Gibbs Racing
126,000 square feet
Fabrication facility: insulated precast concrete and steel frame
Corporate pavilion: curved precast concrete and steel frame, aluminum and glass curtain wall system

Joe Gibbs Racing Facility

Joe Gibbs' new NASCAR (National Association for Stock Car Automobile Racing) facility is sited on a 14-acre tract in Huntersville Business Park. Gibbs' commitment to making significant improvements to its motor sports facility led to the evolution from a small, leased shop of 34,000 square feet to a new, high-tech corporate facility that accommodates three goals: sustaining R&D production, providing a destination point for fans, and meeting the demands of corporate sponsors. The goal of the project was not only to house all these functions under one roof, but also to provide a facility that reflects the ever-growing advancements in technology, which exemplifies the new direction that automobile racing is headed.

The public entrance of the facility, the corporate pavilion, is through a shallow two-story atrium with floor-to-ceiling glass on the entrance side and trophy cases on the interior walls. Race cars for each team are on display. The atrium was designed, in plan, to allude to Joe Gibbs' previous career as football coach of the Washington Redskins. From the atrium, fans have

access to a viewing gallery overlooking the 30,000 square-foot prep shop in the adjoining fabrication facility. From this view, fans can watch the entirety of the prep shop operations, complete with video explainers. Additionally, from the atrium, corporate sponsors have easy entry to the 100-seat stepped theater/auditorium. Sponsors use the facility for corporate events planned in conjunction with race weekends in Charlotte. In a more typical schedule, the individual race teams use the auditorium for training exercises, meetings and Gibbs' motivational-speaking engagements. Adjacent the auditorium is a dual-function employee break room/catering kitchen. The second floor of the pavilion houses the corporate offices.

The 86,000 square-foot production, R&D and fabrication facility is located a level below the ground floor of the pavilion, providing a backdrop for the more visually appealing corporate functions. Included in this fabrication facility are a 10,000 square-foot machine shop with 3-D computer lathe machinery, a 10,000 square-foot integrated testing facility housing a dynacam, and other individual testing components along with a paint shop, body shop and prep shop. Other amenities include an employee athletic facility with a gym, lockers and showers.

1   Two-story entry atrium and team display
2   Pit practice wall at service court
3   Public entry at corporate pavilion at night
Images: Rick Alexander & Associates, Inc.

4 Prep shop with viewing gallery beyond
5 Stepped auditorium/theater used for corporate
   sponsors, motivational speaking engagements and
   team meetings
Images: Rick Alexander & Associates, Inc.

4

5

6

6   Entry atrium at corporate pavilion, at night
Opposite:
    Detail of clerestory at entry atrium
Images: Rick Alexander & Associates, Inc.

1   Front façade

2

1   Front façade
2   View from north at dusk
3   Auditorium
4   North lab with views to exterior
Images: Rick Alexander & Associates, Inc.

Design/Completion 1994/1996
Charleston, South Carolina
Medical University of South Carolina
40,000 square feet
Steel structure/concrete shear walls, stucco

Medical University of South Carolina
Storm Eye Institute

The Medical University of South Carolina (MUSC) Storm Eye Institute is one of the leading ophthalmologic institutes in the world. The new addition was needed to provide state-of-the-art research laboratories and administration space including a teaching auditorium. The Storm Eye Institute vertical expansion is a four-story addition to an existing five story building.

The perimeter of the addition was obviously defined by that of the existing building. The need to extend the existing stair towers, the requirement to add shear walls for earthquake resistance, and the existing materials and fenestration were strong design considerations to be incorporated into the overall design. The shear walls were designed as solid concrete elements extending from below ground to the eighth floor to express the verticality of the addition. The proportion of the shear wall and balconies above were developed as illustrative allusions to the slender vertical proportions of the Charleston single houses that surround the MUSC campus. A one-story rusticated base was added to balance the mass of the new addition with the existing structure, as well as to change the mass to a more human scale at the sidewalks.

The four stories of new construction added to the building create a vertical massing and presence that visually anchors not only the southeast corner of the 'Horseshoe', but also the previously incomplete massing of the adjacent Children's Hospital building. The more classical northern façade with its large pediment is not only an allusion to nearby historical buildings but also the original hospital pediment that was partially hidden by the north tower addition several years ago. The large grid of windows on the north, east and west façades are punctuated visually by a large circle that adds visual interest to the elevations while alluding to the 'eye' in the Storm Eye Institute.

4

3

Design/Completion 1996/1997
Charleston, South Carolina
Roper Foundation
4,000 square feet
Steel construction, stucco

Roper Hospital Bratney Atrium

This client's goal was to provide a defined 'Center' for the Oncology Department at Roper Hospital. The requirements were to add a variety of functional areas for oncology patients, family and staff. The purpose of this central atrium is to create gathering places that provide solace amidst the realities of serious illnesses. Some of the gathering places include family rooms, a consultation room and a resource center. There are also adjacent laundry, restroom, shower and kitchen facilities for use by families.

The focal point of the project is a garden terrace that opens to dramatic views of the historic old city. There is another small 375 square-foot garden patio that acts as a visual buffer and can be viewed by both those in the atrium and several patient rooms. This patio includes a double-sided water feature, which allows the project to be a private garden and a 'good neighbor' for these oncology patients.

There is also another 760 square feet of associated renovations for conference and support spaces as well as new entrance corridors. Every attempt is made to make this oncology atrium as non-institutional as possible. The plan is skewed to create a rotated flooring and ceiling grid that visually breaks away from the more orthogonal grid of the hospital units. The angled, slate-covered entry wall located to one side of the skewed grid creates a welcoming gesture to the visitor while drawing them into the atrium and its garden terrace view to the city beyond.

The atrium spaces are residential in character to create a comfortable oasis for the patients and their families, located, psychologically, far from the unpleasant realities of their illnesses and the medical necessities of the hospital itself. As the dedication plaque eloquently states: 'The Bratney Atrium has been created to offer Respite, Healing, and Hope for our Patients, Family and Friends. We invite you to experience it as a place of peace and renewal'.

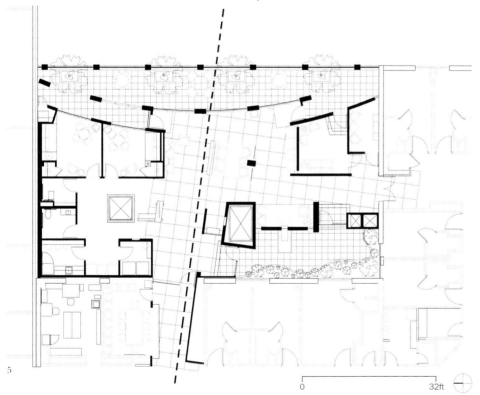

5

0   32ft

1   View to water feature at eating area
2   View to atrium and terrace beyond
3   Reception area and mission statement wall
4   Terrace
5   Floor plan
Images: Rick Alexander & Associates, Inc. (1–4);
LS3P ASSOCIATES LTD. (5)

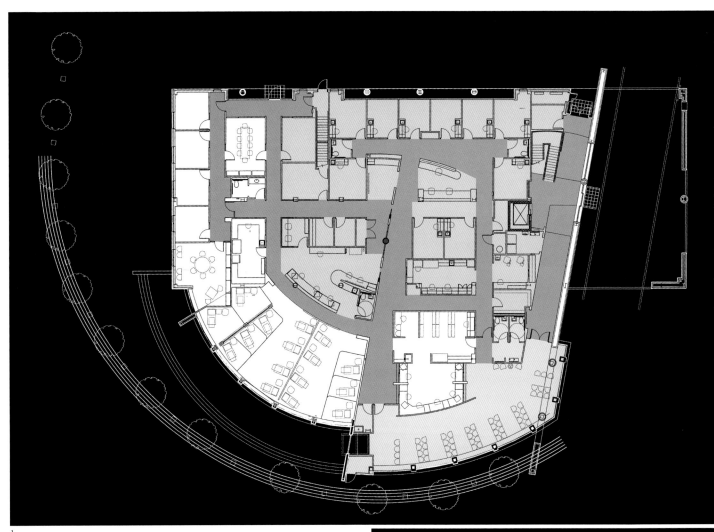

1

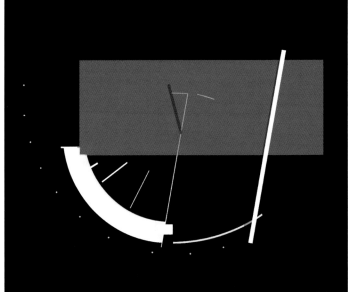

2

1 Floor plan
2 Conceptual plan diagram
3 Axonometric
Images: LS3P ASSOCIATES LTD.

234

Design/Completion 2000/2002
North Charleston, South Carolina
Developer: The PrimeSouth Group
Owner: Jass, Inc.
25,000 square feet
Steel frame, aluminum metal panels, brick, stucco

Trident Palmetto Hematology Oncology Clinic

This 25,000 square-foot medical office building houses 15,000 square feet for an oncology and chemotherapy clinic and 10,000 square feet for tenant medical offices. The design strives to create a forceful vocabulary that speaks of both trustworthy medical practices and the up-to-the-minute technology advances of the profession.

The exterior is a combination of forms and materials that interplay to bring both these ideas of medical treatment to mind. A two-story brick box creates a first impression of a solidly-rooted entry that is bisected by a precast monolith. The angled monolith gives a dynamic inside/outside relationship and it in turn is punctured by 'technology-driven' glass/aluminum panel curved forms. These more translucent forms are the actual patient areas.

The focal point of the patient areas is a 1,000 square-foot reflecting pool that is fed by a double-sided water wall. As the patient progresses through these forms for their particular treatment they are immersed in a healing, 'zen-like' environment, one that uses light, color, volume and water to create the serene surroundings so needed to promote well-being.

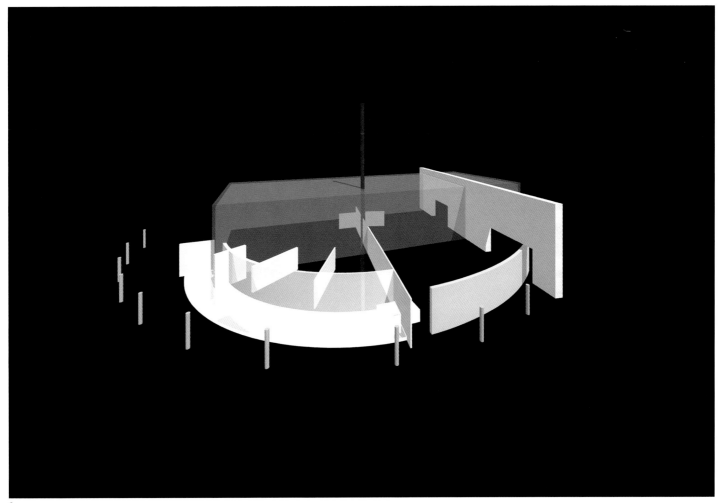

3

Design/Completion 1995/1999
Charleston, South Carolina
Westvaco Chemical Division of Westvaco Corporation
95,195 square feet
Structural steel frame, precast concrete panels, corrugated and insulated metal panels

Westvaco Charleston Technical Center

Opposite:
  Dawn view of entry
2   First floor plan
Images: Rick Alexander & Associates, Inc. (opposite);
LS3P ASSOCIATES LTD. (2)

Rising from the Lowcountry marshes and within the context of an industrial site, this research facility with a three-story atrium link connects a two-story applied research laboratory wing and a three-story research laboratory wing. The massing for the building was derived from the client's adjacency requirements for labs in each division. Each required 18 modules but varied in arrangement. Linked by a three-story atrium that includes the common visitor reception area and a dining area, the design encourages interaction between the 280 staff members ranging from managers to scientists to technicians. They share common circulation spines, dining, and meeting areas, office areas, conference rooms, and common materials, management, and testing facilities. New lab adjacencies were generated for areas that were once remotely located. The project also features numerous specialty labs and includes various levels of constant humidity rooms for analyzing paper samples.

Activities in the facility range from research and development of papers, packaging, composite surfaces, inks, specialty coatings, dye dispersants, asphalt additives, cement and concrete additives, to bleaching processes, agricultural chemicals, paper chemicals, and activated carbons.

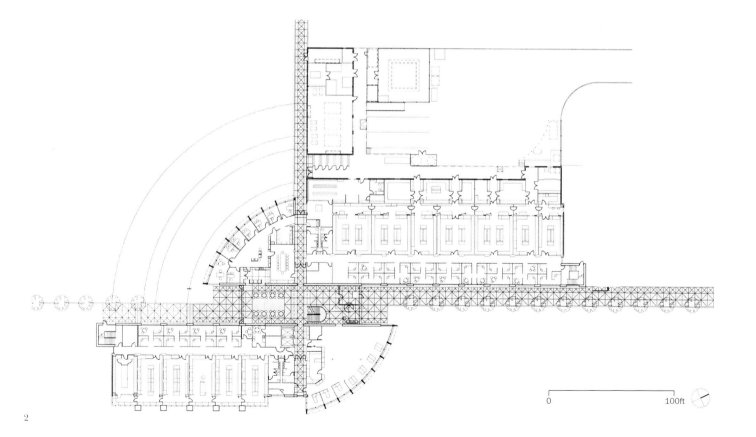

0   100ft

2

3

3 Overview of building and context
4 Interior/exterior relationship at lobby
Opposite:
    Atrium stair and lunchroom
Images: Rick Alexander & Associates, Inc.
(4, opposite); Dickson Dunlap Studios (3)

4

1

1   Transgenic Plant Growth Chamber, Phase IV,
    north entry canopy
2   Transgenic Plant Growth Chamber, Phase IV,
    circulation corridor to growth chambers
3   Transgenic Plant Growth Chamber, Phase IV,
    plant agriculture headhouse
Images: Rick Alexander & Associates, Inc.

Design/Completion 1980/1997 in four phases
Summerville, South Carolina
Westvaco Corporation
64,560 square feet in four phases
Phases I, II, III: wood construction
Phase IV: steel construction
Wood cladding, stucco, aluminum panels

Westvaco Forest Research Complex

Nestled into a forest of pine, the Forest Science Research Building is a poetic metaphor uniting form with function. This complex encompasses an original 27,700 square feet (Biotechnology I) and four subsequent additions for a total project of 64,560 square feet. Both the original facility and later additions were designed to celebrate the client's forest science research as well as the pine forest setting surrounding the building.

The original building and Biotechnology addition (Phase II) added research laboratories and administrative offices. Biotechnology II (Phase III) added seven additional laboratories, auxiliary administrative offices and conference space.

Phase IV, the Transgenic Plant Growth Chamber Facility is an 18,000 square-foot addition that houses ten controlled growth chambers that supplement the biotechnology research. The mechanical functions of the chambers vary from walk-in cold rooms to lighted/dark growth environments.

2

3

4

4   Biotechnology II addition, Phase III, visiting
     scientist office
5   Laboratory complex, Phase I, main campus
     entry/administration
6   Biotechnology II addition, Phase III,
     administrative/conference facilities
Images: Rick Alexander & Associates, Inc. (4,6);
Gordon H. Schenck, Jr. Photography (5)

5   6

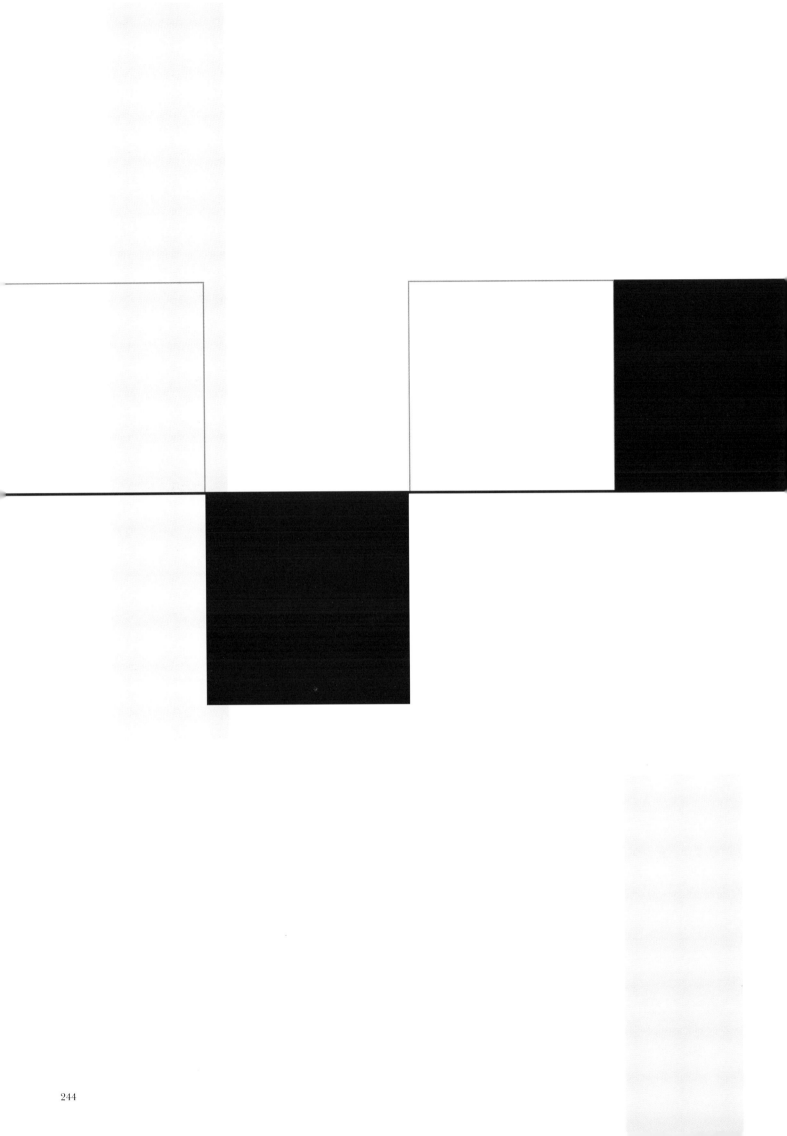

FIRM PROFILE

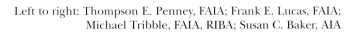

Left to right: Thompson E. Penney, FAIA; Frank E. Lucas, FAIA; Michael Tribble, FAIA, RIBA; Susan C. Baker, AIA

Principals and Associates

Board of Directors

Frank E. Lucas, FAIA
Chairman

Michael Tribble, FAIA, RIBA
Vice Chairman

Thompson E. Penney, FAIA
President & Chief Executive Officer

Susan C. Baker, AIA
Chief Operating Officer

Principals

Eric C. Aichele, AIA
Roger M. Attanasio, AIA
Richard D. Bartlett, AIA
Byron M. Edwards III, AIA
Jeffrey C. Floyd, AIA
Thomas J. Hund, AIA
Christopher G. Ions, AIA
Samuel S. Logan III, AIA
John L. Mack
Barbara M. Price, AIA
W. Warren Pruitt Jr., ASLA
George E. Temple IV, AIA
James M. Williams Jr., AIA
Cameron L. Wilson, IIDA

Officers

William Scott Baker, AIA
David A. Creech, AIA
Margaret L. Lowder, ASID

Senior Associates

Richard C. Bing, AIA
D. Patterson Campbell
Nina M. Fair, AIA, CCS
Richard J. Gowe, AIA
Kenneth E. Harkins, AIA
Rodger F. Hinton, AIA
Steven A. Hurr, AIA
Burneil L. Lindquist, RA
David O. Loy, AIA
Steven L. Meyer, AIA
Willie W. Murphy, AIA
John P. Reuter, AIA
David L. Rice, AIA
Rebecca M. Smith, AIA
Lyudmila Sobchuk, AIA
Allen R. Taylor, AIA

Associates

Janette Alexander, RA
Donald E. Baus
David A. Bellamy, AIA
Brian Bresg, AIA
Mark G. Clancy, AIA
Gary G. Collins, ASLA
Steven C. Diesing, RA
Lisa C. Gomperts, AIA
Delores D. Harris
Paul D. Hartley, AIA
David P. Hutcheson, AIA
Gregory A. Kenner
Joseph T. Monico, AIA
Shawn K. Mottern
Kristin G. Mulkey
Connie Myers
Craig E. Norsted, AIA
Brian L. Tressler
Wade A. Tucker
Brian Wurst

Collaborators

Jason Aaron

James Doug Anderson

Timothy J. Bass, CDT, CCCA

F. Casey Bearsch

Kenneth O. Bolin, AIA

Charles W. Boyce

Kristi Brown

William G. Bullock Jr

Susan M. Burke

David C. Burt

Tracy L. Cain

Karen K. Cecil

Joseph E. Chaffee

A. Todd Chambers

Lea Clement

Mary E. Corbett

Hamilton Cort

Charlotte J. Cox

John Crawford

Sandrine Danielson

April R. Davidson

Rebecca Dugan

Thomas Eline

E. Berkeleigh Fisher

Brent Fleming

Rita Forthofer

Craig N. Galow

Mary Ellen George

Judith R. Gilbert

Uai Godwin

Jennifer B. Granger

Fredrick Guthier

Julia H. Hall, CSI, CCS

Samuel Halverson

Scott A. Harvey

Cynthia Kaye Hoagland

Roni E. Holland

Charlean J. Horne

Scott Howell

Donald S. Hughes, AIA

Jennifer Jackson

Carsyn L. Jarrell

Rochelle Johnson

Paul Joseph

Krista Karlson

Krista Karlson

Jonathon B. Kincheloe, AIA

Betty H. Kunreuther

Cecilia Leary

Rodrigo E. Letonja

Aletha R. Lindquist

Kathy Litton

Daniel H. Marchant

Leigh A. Martin

Kym McLean

Andrew E. McLellan

Catherine S. Meyer

Richard Molony

Anthony Morlando, AIA

Sharon A. Murray

Angela Navy

Denise V. Norsted

Lauren C. Oller

Russell Pound

Michael Romot

Steve G. Schwaeber, AIA

Jackie Shedrow

Fred Henry Shute II

Bradley Sikes

Julie A. Smith

Megan Smith

Gregory Soyka, AIA

Sharon Stevens

G. Bryant Stowe, ASLA

Gregory Strickland

Mary Szvetecz

Dennis C. Terry, ASLA

Elizabeth Tolley

David H. Tomblin, ASLA

Alicia Tomkinson

Nilgun Trogdon

Dawn Van Dyke, IIDA

Kelly M. Walker

Lynn A. Warne

L. Anthony Waters

Meghan B. West

Killough H. White, AIA

Kenneth Wiley

Awards

Individual Achievement Awards

Thompson E. Penney, FAIA
2003
President, American Institute of Architects

Thompson E. Penney, FAIA
2002
First Vice President, President Elect, American Institute of Architects

Michael Tribble, FAIA, RIBA
2000
Elected to the College of Fellows of the American Institute of Architects
Category: Design

Frank E. Lucas, FAIA
1997
Medal of Distinction, South Carolina Chapter, American Institute of Architects

Frank E. Lucas, FAIA
1996
Joseph P. Riley Leadership Award
Charleston Trident Chamber of Commerce

Michael Tribble, FAIA, RIBA
1996
President
School of Design Foundation, North Carolina State University

Thompson E. Penney, FAIA
1990
Elected to the College of Fellows of the American Institute of Architects
Category: Design

Michael Tribble, FAIA, RIBA
1988
Elected into Corporate membership of the Royal Institute of British Architects

Frank E. Lucas, FAIA
1983
Elected to the College of Fellows of the American Institute of Architects
Category: Design, Preservation, Service to Profession, Service to Public

Firm Awards

1995
25-Year Medal of Distinction
South Carolina Chapter, American Institute of Architects

1993
Best Collaborative Partnership Award in Recognition of Voluntary Efforts in Enriching the Lives of Young Americans, Navy Personal Excellence Partnership of the Year
Commander, Naval Base, Charleston, South Carolina

1989
Business Category, Elizabeth O'Neill Verner Governor's Award for the Arts
South Carolina Arts Commission

1989
Partnership Award, South Carolina Business and the Arts
South Carolina Joint Legislative Committee on Cultural Affairs and South Carolina Arts Foundation

1984
Silver Medal for Distinction in Design, Tau Sigma Delta Architectural Honor Society, Clemson University

1984
'20 Years of Design Excellence'
Gibbs Museum of Art, Charleston, South Carolina

1964
First Place, Design Competition
Gaillard Municipal Auditorium and Exhibition Hall, Charleston, South Carolina

Project Awards

AXA Berryhill
2001
Merit Award
Carolinas Chapter, The American Society of Interior Designers

Ballantyne, CBP-1H, Pinkerton Building
2001
Certificate of Special Recognition
Outstanding use of precast, prestressed concrete components
Precast/Prestressed Concrete Institute

Banks Construction Company
1972
National Design Award of Merit
Armco Building Systems, Inc.

Barracks, Dining & Community Facilities
1998
Award for Design Excellence
National Concrete Masonry Association, Landscape Products Group

Battery Creek High School
1994
Brick in Architecture Design Competition Merit Award
South Carolina Brick Association

Bordeleau Apartments
1967
Award for Design Excellence
South Carolina Chapter, American Institute of Architects

Budget Rental Car Sales Center
1985
National Design Award of Merit
Armco Building Systems, Inc.

Carolina First Bank
1998
Carolopolis Awards, Outstanding Achievement in New Construction
Preservation Society of Charleston

Carolina Ice Palace
1999
Retail Honor Award
Carolinas Chapter, The American Society of Interior Designers

Charleston County Health Complex, Parking Garage and EMS Station
1997
Citation
South Carolina Chapter, American Institute of Architects
1996
Spring Convention & Design Conference, People's Choice Award—First Place
South Carolina Chapter, American Institute of Architects
1994
Special Recognition
Precast/Prestressed Concrete Institute

Charleston Gateway Center
1999
Gold Award, IIDA Spaces 1999 Professional Design Competition
International Interior Design Association
1998
Second Place
Carolinas Chapter, The American Society of Interior Designers

Charleston Trident Chamber of Commerce
1993
Carolopolis Awards, Outstanding Achievement in Rehabilitation
Preservation Society of Charleston

Charlotte Chamber of Commerce Building
1996
Renovation/Addition, First Place
Charlotte-Mecklenburg Community Enhancement Award

College of Charleston Fine Arts Center
1980
Award for Design Excellence
South Carolina Chapter, American Institute of Architects

Commissioners of Public Works Administrative Offices
1989
South Carolina Energy Awards
1986
Builder's Choice Awards Competition
Builder Magazine
1985
Aurora Award
Southeast Builder's Conference
1988
Award for Design Excellence
South Carolina Chapter, American Institute of Architects
1987
Professional Design Award
Precast/Prestressed Concrete Institute

Commonwealth 20 Theatre, Richmond, Virginia
2001
Merit Award
Carolinas Chapter, The American Society of Interior Designers

Conway Riverwalk
1995
Honor Award
South Carolina Chapter of the American Society of Landscape Architects
1993
Best New Construction Project
South Carolina Downtown Development Association

Coosaw Creek
1998
Award, Best Community Presentation

Coosaw Creek Country Club
1999
Bronze Award, IIDA Spaces 1999 Professional Design Competition
International Interior Design Association
1998
Prism Award, Best Landscaping Design
Charleston Trident Home Builders' Association
1998
Second Place
Carolinas Chapter, The American Society of Interior Designers

Country Club of Charleston
1992
Honorable Mention
Institute of Business Designers, Carolinas Chapter

Crestar Riverview Center
1998
Honor Award
North Carolina American Institute of Architects

Crossings Park
1997
Merit Award for Design
South Carolina Chapter of the American Society of Landscape Architects
1995
Merit Award
South Carolina Chapter of the American Society of Landscape Architects

Deas Hall, The Citadel
1978
Award for Design Excellence
South Carolina Chapter, American Institute of Architects

Dorchester County Library
1980
Award for Design Excellence
South Carolina Chapter, American Institute of Architects

Downtown Myrtle Beach Redevelopment Plan
1995
Merit Award
South Carolina Chapter of the American Society of Landscape Architects

East Bay Community Center
1980
Award for Design Excellence
South Carolina Chapter, American Institute of Architects

Estill Federal Correctional Institution
1996
Award for Design Excellence
South Carolina Chapter, American Institute of Architects
1996
Justice Facilities Review
American Institute of Architects

Firehouse Sixteen
1986
Award for Design Excellence
South Carolina Chapter, American Institute of Architects

First Federal Savings and Loan West Side Office
1982
Award for Design Excellence
South Carolina Chapter, American Institute of Architects

First Union National Bank Regional Banking Center
1992
Award for Design Excellence
South Carolina Chapter, American Institute of Architects

Fort Benning, GA Receptee Barracks
1988
Award for Design Excellence
South Carolina Chapter, American Institute of Architects

Fort Bragg, NC JFK Special Warfare Center
1993
Special Recognition
Precast/Prestressed Concrete Institute

Fort Stewart, GA Bachelor Officers' Quarters
1981
Honorable Mention, Design & Environmental Awards Competition
United States Army Corps of Engineers

Freedom Florence Recreation Complex
1992
Honor Award
Charleston Section, American Institute of Architects
1991
Achievement Award
South Carolina Municipal Association's, 51st Annual Meeting, Charleston, South Carolina
1990
Facilities Award
Softball Owners and Directors of America, Annual Conference, El Paso, Texas

Gaillard Municipal Auditorium and Exhibition Hall
1970
Award for Design Excellence
South Carolina Chapter, American Institute of Architects

Gaillard Municipal Parking Garage
1996
Honorable Mention
International Parking Institute

Harbor View Station West Cinemas Suffolk, Virginia
2001
Award of Merit
Best Commercial/Retail Building 20,000-100,000 square feet
Hampton Roads Association for Commercial Real Estate

Henry J. Lee Distributors, Inc.
1980
National Design Award of Merit
Armco Building Systems, Inc.

Hollings and Hawkins Law Offices
1974
Award for Design Excellence
South Carolina Chapter, American Institute of Architects

Hotel Roanoke Renovation
1995
Award of Excellence
Architectural Woodwork Institute

J.M. Huber Wood Products Division
1998
Merit Award
North Carolina American Institute of Architects
1998
Honor Award for Excellence in Interior Design
Virginia American Institute of Architects
Inform Magazine
1997
Honor Award
Charlotte Chapter, American Institute of Architects

Julian Mitchell Elementary School
1994
Award of Recognition, Brick in Architecture Design Competition

South Carolina Brick Association
1993
Carolopolis Awards, Outstanding Achievement in Preservation
Preservation Society of Charleston
1993
Carolopolis Awards, Outstanding Achievement in New Construction
Preservation Society of Charleston

Kiawah Island Sales and Information Center
1996
Spring Convention & Design Conference, People's Choice Award - Second Place
South Carolina Chapter, American Institute of Architects
1990
Gold Award, Office, Offices Under 25,000 square feet
Institute of Business Designers, Carolinas Chapter
1990
Bronze Award, Office, Best of Show
Institute of Business Designers, Carolinas Chapter

Kings Bay, GA Enlisted Dining Facility
1988
Award for Design Excellence
South Carolina Chapter, American Institute of Architects

Laurel Bay Whole House Repairs, Marine Corps Air Station, Beaufort, South Carolina
1990
Certificate of Appreciation
Naval Facilities Engineering Command

Lower Dorchester County Recreation Needs Assessment Master Plan
1993
Merit Award
South Carolina Chapter of the American Society of Landscape Architects

Mauldin Middle School
2001
Gold Award, Education Forum, IIDA Spaces 2001 Professional Design Competition, International Interior Design Association

Medical University of South Carolina Storm Eye Institute
1999
Silver Award, IIDA Spaces 1999 Professional Design Competition
International Interior Design Association
1999
Merit Award for Vertical Addition
Carolinas Chapter, The American Society of Interior Designers

Naval Air Station Pensacola, FL, CNET Technical Training Complex
1995
Certificate of Appreciation
Naval Facilities Engineering Command

Ness Motley Loadholt Richardson & Poole Law Offices
2001
Honor Award
Carolinas Chapter, The American Society of Interior Designers

Newton Office Building
2000
Honor Award
Carolinas Chapter, The American Society of Interior Designers

North Charleston Convention Center
2000
Honor Award
Carolinas Chapter, The American Society of
Interior Designers

North Charleston Performing Arts Center
2000
Merit Award
Carolinas Chapter, The American Society of
Interior Designers

Palmetto Grande Cinemas
2000
Honor Award
Carolinas Chapter, The American Society of
Interior Designers

Phillips Place
2001
Certificate of Merit for Innovative Design and
Construction of a New Center
International Design and Development Awards
International Council of Shopping Centers

Piggly Wiggly Corporate Headquarters Suite
2000
Honor Award
Carolinas Chapter, The American Society of
Interior Designers
2000
Honor Award Specialty Custom Furniture
Design
Carolinas Chapter, The American Society of
Interior Designers

Pilgrim II
1995
Merit Award for Design Excellence, Contract
Design—Corporate
Carolinas Chapter, The American Society of
Interior Designers

Pontiac Elementary School
1992
Honor Award
Charleston Section, American Institute of
Architects
1992
Brick in Architecture Design Competition
President's Award
South Carolina Brick Association

Pope Air Force Base Dormitory Complex
1999
Airmobility Command Concept Design Award
Department of the Air Force, Air Mobility
Command

Preserve at Indigo Run
2001
Gold Award, Hospitality Forum, IIDA Spaces
2001 Professional Design Competition
International Interior Design Association

Riverbanks Zoo Farm Building
1996
Award for Design Excellence
South Carolina Chapter, American Institute of
Architects

Roper Hospital Bratney Atrium
1999
Gold Award, IIDA Spaces 1999 Professional
Design Competition
International Interior Design Association
1999
Second Best of Show, IIDA Spaces 1999
Professional Design Competition

International Interior Design Association
1998
Citation for Healthcare Facilities Design
AIA/Modern Healthcare

Roper Hospital Interdenominational Chapel
1997
Special Award for Interiors
South Carolina Chapter, American Institute of
Architects

Roper Hospital Oncology
1998
Honorable Mention
Carolinas Chapter, The American Society of
Interior Designers

Saks Fifth Avenue/Majestic Square
2000
Merit Award
South Atlantic Regional Council, American
Institute of Architects
1998
First Place
Carolinas Chapter, The American Society of
Interior Designers
1998
Honor Award
South Carolina Brick Association
1998
People's Choice Design Award
Charleston Section, American Institute of
Architects

Saluda Trail Middle School
2000
Honor Award
Carolinas Chapter, The American Society of
Interior Designers

**Sangaree Intermediate School, Berkeley County,
South Carolina**
1989
Design Award
Carolina Concrete Masonry Association

**South Carolina Public Service Authority
Transportation Service Center**
1984
Award for Design Excellence
South Carolina Chapter, American Institute of
Architects

Southend Brewery
1998
Award for Design Excellence
South Carolina Chapter, American Institute of
Architects

Tamassee Salem Middle/High School
2000
Merit Award
South Atlantic Regional Council, American
Institute of Architects
1999
Award for Design Excellence
South Carolina Chapter, American Institute of
Architects

Tea Farm Park
1996
Unbuilt Category Merit Award for Interpretive
Center
South Carolina Chapter, American Institute of
Architects
1995
Historical Preservation Project, Second Annual
Competition
Public Landscapes of America

**The Historic Charleston Foundation Retail
Offices**
1992
Special Award, Historic Preservation
South Carolina Chapter, American Institute of
Architects

The Penney House
1985
Aurora Award
Southeast Builder's Conference
1980
Award for Design Excellence
South Carolina Chapter, American Institute of
Architects
1980
Award for Design Excellence
South Atlantic Regional Council, American
Institute of Architects

The Ronald McDonald House of Charleston
1984
Award for Design Excellence
South Carolina Chapter, American Institute of
Architects
1984
Aurora Award
Southeast Builder's Conference
1984
Grand Award, Builder's Choice Awards
Competition
Builder Magazine

Tidewater Swim and Racquet Club
1993
Merit Award
South Carolina Chapter of the American Society
of Landscape Architects

Volvo Truck Administration Building
2000
Merit Award
Carolinas Chapter, The American Society of
Interior Designers

Wall Street Capitol Interiors
2001
Gold Award, Commercial Forum, IIDA Spaces
2001 Professional Design Competition
International Interior Design Association

Westvaco Forest Research Complex
1998
First Place for Research Facility Addition
Carolinas Chapter, The American Society of
Interior Designers
1986
Award for Design Excellence
South Carolina Chapter, American Institute of
Architects
1984
Award for Design Excellence
South Carolina Chapter, American Institute of
Architects
1984
Laboratory of the Year—High Honors
Research and Development
1983
Aurora Award
Southeast Builder's Conference

Acknowledgments

LS3P is grateful to those involved in the extraordinary preparation of this documentation of the history of our firm, and the presentation of the representative showing of its work. Mike Tribble accepted the task of overall responsibility, and Margaret Lowder was the person who made it all come together. Their persistence made it happen.

Our particular appreciation is to those clients, consultants, and to all those talented individuals and professionals without whom this firm could not exist. It is the constant dedication and support above and beyond duty by our employees and associates that have allowed LS3P to excel as a local, state, and now as a regional design firm, poised to accept all new opportunities and challenges.

We are proud of the achievements and recognition received by our clients, our projects, and our truly exceptional staff. The satisfaction of providing a significant role in the growth and development of our clients' business and professional programs and objectives is indeed heartwarming and gratifying.

The first 40 years of LS3P have been monumental, with steady growth from a simple beginning to a vibrant and exciting multi-faceted firm. We are committed to our profession, our staff, our clients, and our future.

Frank E. Lucas, FAIA
Chairman
LS3P ASSOCIATES LTD.

Index

The information and illustrations in this publication has been prepared and supplied by LS3P ASSOCIATES LTD. While all reasonable efforts have been made to ensure accuracy, the publishers do not, under any circumstances, accept responsibility for errors, omissions and representations express or implied.